The Vincent Family Diary

Gentry life in Victorian Bangor

by
Dennis S. Wood
and
Vanessa Field

First published in 2002

ISBN 1 84220 029 1

Published in association with
The Marketing and Public Relations Office
University of Wales, Bangor

Printed by W.O. Jones Ltd
Llangefni, Ynys Mon
LL77 7EH

CONTENTS

ACKNOWLEDGEMENTS

The authors gratefully record their appreciation to the many descendants of the Vincent family, without whose kindness and interest, this book could not have been written. We are especially indebted for their hospitality and generosity in the loan of photographs, letters and family papers. Their encouragement has maintained our enthusiasm.

They are:

the late Allan James Vincent Arthur, MBE, DL of Chelmsford, Essex, grandson of Sir William Vincent, and his son, Charles Vincent Arthur of Camberwell, London;

Mrs Bronwen Armitage of Tarporley, Cheshire, Mrs Audrey Wastell of Winchmore Hill, London, and the Rev. Tom Vincent Overton, formerly the rector of Leigh, near Tonbridge, Kent, grandchildren of Sir Hugh Vincent;

Mrs Anne Eastham of Fishguard, great-grand-daughter of James Edmund Vincent;

Lt. Col. John Lloyd-Williams, MC, DL, of Birmingham, grandson of Ellen Lloyd-Williams (née Vincent) and his son Simon Vincent Lloyd-Williams of Talybont, near Aberystwyth;

Mrs Philippa Heather of Abingdon, near Oxford, grand-daughter of Grace Georgiana Hudson (née Vincent) and Dr Sir Richard Lynch-Blosse of Dorchester-on-Thames, great-grandson of 'Georgie' Hudson, and owner of Mollie Vincent's diaries and many of the earlier Vincent papers and documents.

We are also grateful to the following for their generous assistance:

Sir Kyffin Williams RA, for the loan of family photograph albums and many stimulating conversations; Sir Timothy and Lady Mary Colman for their kind hospitality at Bixley Manor, Norwich, and access to the photograph albums of Sir Timothy's grandmother, Edith Colman (née Davies); Tomos Roberts, Elen Wyn Hughes and Diana Clark of the Department of Manuscripts, University of Wales, Bangor, for improving the efficiency of our researches and providing access to photographs in the university collection; Dr Brigid Allen, the Archivist of Jesus College Oxford; Robin Adams, Deputy Librarian of Trinity College,

Dublin; the staff of Gwynedd Archives Service in Caernarfon and Dolgellau, and the Anglesey Archives in Llangefni; Edmund Bailey of Corsygedol, Dyffryn, near Harlech, for welcoming us to his home; Vida Lloyd-Jones of Cwmbran, for providing what we long despaired of finding, a photograph of the long-demolished Caernarfon vicarage, where so many of the Vincent children were born; John Payne, Registrar and Archivist of Christ College, Brecon; Joan Franklin, former secretary at Moreton Hall School for providing vital leads and connections; Douglas Madge for the generous loan of photographic equipment and technical assistance; John Cowell for access to his extensive collection of postcards of nineteenth-century Bangor; Professor Peter Field for reading the manuscript and many helpful suggestions; Lizzie Field for always being there to solve problems with the computer, and Catherine Field for the countless times she put on the kettle.

Dennis Wood
Vanessa Field

Vanessa Field also wishes to thank the University of Wales Guild of Graduates for a research grant, and John Wynne Jones of the Marketing and Public Relations Office of the University of Wales, Bangor, Paul Rayner, and Terry Williams for their help in bringing this book to publication.

FOREWORD

by

Sir Kyffin Williams RA

The important part played by the Anglo-Welsh in the recent history of Wales is often forgotten and, if remembered, is frequently denigrated: nevertheless, their work in the Church, in the law and in the preservation of our landscape contributed enormously to our country as a whole. Without their financial help few books written in Welsh would have been published during the eighteenth and nineteenth centuries.

Although I am Welsh by birth, and born of Welsh-speaking parents, it was into an Anglo-Welsh society that I grew up. One of my great-great-grandmothers was a Vincent of Bangor and descended from the Anglo-Welsh Corbets of Ynysymaengwyn; so the Vincents were related to me and I knew many of them when I was a boy.

At the age of six I went to school at Moreton Hall, a girls' school founded by my cousin Lil Lloyd-Williams, whose maiden name was Vincent. I remember her two brothers, Sir Hugh Vincent, a lawyer and Wales' first rugby scrum-half, and Sir William, his younger brother, who, as Head of an Indian Civil Service department, drew up in 1917 a plan for the self-government of India, a project that he believed should have taken place over thirty years. I knew the Davies family of Treborth, the Wynne-Joneses of Treiorwerth and the Ramsays, who were my father's first cousins. Their father made the first geological survey of Wales, and their names and those of the Davies and Wynne-Jones families appear often in the Diaries. Another name that is often mentioned is that of Rathbone, a philanthropic family that did so much to see that the University College of Bangor was founded with a sound financial structure.

These families, all comparatively wealthy, devoted their lives to serving the communities in Anglesey and Caernarvonshire. It is fitting that this book should record their contribution, for it was a valuable one, and one that could so easily have been forgotten.

The Vincent Family c.1870. Mrs Grace Vincent, widow of Rev. James Crawley Vincent, and her children (clockwise from top left) Edmund, Hugh, Mollie holding Georgie, Lil, Evangeline, William and Augustus on his mother's lap.

INTRODUCTION

This is the story of a Victorian family named Vincent who lived in North Wales. It is also, in part, a two-year chronicle of a widowed mother and her eight children. To their contemporaries they were probably an unexceptional gentry family, respectable but far from wealthy, church-going and educated. From a modern perspective, however, their history and now largely forgotten achievements appear far more remarkable. Though deeply rooted in Wales, the Vincents were the product of a rich and broad genetic amalgam. Theirs was a truly British pedigree. They were the proud possessors of an eminent line of Norman descent which through several generations of marriage became predominantly Welsh. To this had been added earlier Saxon elements and a later injection of both Irish and Huguenot blood. The Norman descent is traced back to King Edward I of England. The principal Welsh line of ancestry derives, over 22 generations, directly from Gruffydd ap Cynan, King of Wales 1079-1137, and his son Owain Gwynedd, Prince of North Wales born in 1100, to the Vincent children, born in the middle of the nineteenth century, who are the subject of this book.

*

On February 14th 1878, Grace Elizabeth Vincent and her eight children took possession of a modest manor house situated three miles from the centre of the small Welsh cathedral city of Bangor, in the then county of Carnarvonshire. The house, Treborth Uchaf, dating back to at least 1470, sat in an estate of the same name comprising 150 acres of park land and wooded coverts running down to the shore of the Menai Straits on the mainland bank. The property had been bequeathed to Grace Vincent's eldest daughter, Mary Matilda, then aged 18, and would pass into her legal ownership when she came of age in 1880. It was to be home to Mary – often known as Mollie – for the next 74 years.

It was the first house that this mid-Victorian generation of the Vincent family had owned. Grace and her husband, the Reverend James Crawley Vincent, Vicar of Caernarfon, had, with their ever-enlarging family, spent the last ten years of their fifteen-year marriage at the vicarage of Llanbeblig. The vicarage and its gardens stood on part of the visible remains of the Roman fortress of Segontium, and commanded fine panoramic views over Caernarfon with its castle, the mountains of Snowdonia to the east and the more topographically subdued island county of Anglesey to the west. The untimely death of James Crawley Vincent at the age of 42 in 1869, left Grace not only with eight children between the ages of 12 years and 1 year, but also necessitated her vacating the family home. Through the offices of the Church and notably of Grace Vincent's father-in-law, James Vincent, who was the Dean of Bangor, the family moved into a house on a steep and winding lane linking upper and lower Bangor. The house was near to the Cathedral Close, the Bishop's Palace and the Deanery.

At the time the family moved to Bangor, the two eldest boys, James Edmund (Ted, born 1857) and Hugh Corbet (born 1863) were already away at school. Shortly before his father's death, Ted had won scholarships to both Eton and Winchester and had chosen Winchester. Hugh, a fine boy soprano, went to Worcester Cathedral Choir School. The other children were Mary Matilda (Mollie, born 1859), Ellen Augusta Crawley (Lil, born 1860), Evangeline Margaret (Eva, born 1864), William Henry Hoare (Will, born 1866), Grace Georgiana Wynne (Georgie, born 1867), and Augustus Edward (Gustie, born 1868).

Treborth Uchaf,
as it looks today

Though living in reasonable comfort, a secure future for the family was assured by the bequest to them of the Treborth Uchaf estate. The Venerable Edmund Jones Crawley, Prebendary of Bath and Wells, was cousin to the children's grandmother, Margaret Matilda Vincent (née Crawley), the late wife of Dean James Vincent. As the children were Margaret Matilda's only grandchildren, it was perhaps understandably generous, that on his death in 1871, the Prebendary left the property, which he himself had inherited not long before, to provide the fatherless family with both income and a home. The legacy went to the eldest daughter, Mollie, in order to ensure the property stayed within the family, given the possibility that Grace, then aged 43, might remarry.

In 1871, there was a tenant living and farming at Treborth Uchaf with six years still to run on a 21-year tenancy. Mollie was only 12 years old, so a trust was established on her behalf and administered by her grandfather, the Dean, pending her 21st birthday. Upon expiry of the existing tenancy in 1877 and after extension of the house, the family prepared to move to Treborth.

The Vincents took up residence at their new home on St Valentine's Day of the following year, 1878. Ted, now 20, was in his second term at Christ Church, Oxford; Hugh was 15 and at school at Sherborne in Dorset; the others were at home and ranged in age from 18 to 9. They had lived in Bangor for eight years and in that period the older members of the family had developed a wide circle of friends. Grace was well connected through the Church and the family regularly attended worship at Bangor Cathedral. Grace also took a keen interest in politics. This and the children's recreational activities ensured that the entire family was happily established in local society. The younger members grew up in an easy and seemingly carefree world of country pursuits and many friendships. It was an active life of the sea and the mountains, of sailing and rowing, of tennis and cricket, rambling and hunting. It was also a cultural life enriched by music, the theatre and the conversation of its tea parties. The home was a happy one in which relatives and friends were always welcomed, and to which all of the children would regularly return. Their life-style is vividly encapsulated in the Family Diary kept by Mollie Vincent, which includes contributions from her brothers and sisters either when she was absent, or when they had particular experiences to relate.

Two volumes only survive. They are for 1885 and 1886, two years which were eventful for both the Vincents and the country. They reveal a world in which life was lived at a more leisurely pace, and was still supported by a confidence perhaps greater than our own. That life, however, was an idyll more apparent than real. National uncertainty about the future was beginning to appear. Such apprehension was hardly dispelled by the fact that in twelve turbulent months between June 1885 and June 1886 there were four changes of Prime Minister. The Vincents occasionally record national concerns, but this is essentially their family record book and as such it concentrates more upon their private activities, family events and joyful occasions. As the family members embarked upon marriage and careers, they had every reason to be confident and optimistic. They could not foresee the tragic event which was to bring the Diary to an abrupt end in the November of 1886.

Authors' Note

Fortunately for the present researchers, Mollie Vincent was a great hoarder of family papers and memorabilia. The Diary, together with its accompanying items remained at Treborth Uchaf until 1952 when all passed into the ownership of the descendants of the last surviving member of the family. It is now the property of Sir Richard Lynch-Blosse of Dorchester-upon-Thames, the great grandson of Grace Georgiana, the youngest of the Vincent sisters. The authors are particularly grateful for his kindness and generosity in allowing free access to the Diary and much primary material.

The illustrations which accompany the book fall into four categories. These comprise the souvenirs which were collected and preserved by Mollie Vincent; contemporary nineteenth-century photographs which have been obtained from members of all the present-day branches of the family and the descendants of family friends; archival materials found in various repositories; and the authors' own photographs of locations and houses which are mentioned in the narrative of the Diary and which remain essentially unaltered to the present day. The trail has entailed visits to churchyards and historic houses, both grand and humble, and the opportunity to meet a large number of delightful people in many parts of England and Wales. For their assistance and hospitality, we extend our sincere thanks.

The Diary is preceded by a family history of the Vincents and a glimpse of some of the more prominent of their friends, together with a picture of the period and environment in which the Diary was written. The Diary itself is annotated only where clarification is thought to be helpful. The book concludes with a biographical review of the subsequent lives and achievements of the Vincent children of Treborth.

All the Vincents, including their mother, contribute to the Diary, except the youngest, Gustie. They usually write in the third person and only a change in handwriting signals a change of writer. From other family papers we have been able to identify the individual contributors. The various family members are inconsistent in their use of 'Mary' and 'Mollie' when referring to their sister, Mary Matilda. She herself uses her formal name, Mary. However, in order to overcome this inconsistency, we have chosen to use 'Mollie' throughout the book. This has the merit of avoiding confusion with her many friends and relatives with the name Mary who appear in the Diary.

Mollie Vincent never married, but to her 25 nephews and nieces and their children, she was always 'Aunt Mollie'. We should like to dedicate this book to her memory.

Captain John Jones (1753-1823) of Pant Howel, Llandegfan, Anglesey, great-grandfather of the Vincent children.

Pant Howel, Llandegfan, Anglesey

Part One: Family Origins

---

1. THE VINCENT FAMILY HISTORY

The Clerical Vincents of Anglesey

Thomas Vincent (1677-1738) was the first of several generations of the family who became priests of the Welsh Church. He effectively founded a dynasty of clerics.[1] Thomas Vincent was educated at Trinity College, Cambridge, where he obtained his M.A. degree in 1698, and then held a College teaching fellowship for several years. He was appointed to the Diocese of Bangor and was Vicar Choral at the Cathedral, prior to becoming Rector of Llanfachraeth in western Anglesey in 1713. In the following year he married Jane Anwyl (1678-1742) of the house of Parc, in the Croesor Valley, approximately six miles due south of the summit of Snowdon. It was the Anwyl family which possessed the auspicious Welsh heritage reaching back from Jane over 16 generations to Owain Gwynedd, Prince of North Wales in the twelfth century.[2]

Thomas Vincent remained Rector of Llanfachraeth for 25 years, during which period his wife bore him four children. The two sons followed their father into the priesthood and one daughter married a priest. The elder son, also Thomas Vincent (1717-1798), attended Jesus College, Oxford, was ordained at Christ Church Cathedral, then held several livings in Anglesey before becoming Archdeacon of Brecon in 1770. The younger son, the Reverend James Vincent (1718-1783), also attended Jesus College, and in 1740 was appointed headmaster of Friars' School, the grammar school which had been founded in the town of Bangor in 1557, on the site of the former Dominican Friary. In 1750 he became Second Canon of Bangor, was Rector of Llanfairfechan from 1753 to 1763, and then, like his father, was Rector of Llanfachraeth from 1763 until his death in 1783. He was also Chancellor of Bangor Cathedral for the last ten years of his life.

The elder Thomas Vincent's daughter, Catherine (1716-1793), married the Reverend Owen Jones who was First Canon of Bangor from 1760 to 1782. They

---

[1] See Appendix 1
[2] See Appendix 2

1

had two sons, the elder of whom entered the Church, whilst his younger brother, John, entered the army and served with the 62nd Regiment during the American War of Independence. Captain John Jones (1753-1823) fought at the Battles of Saratoga, Ticonderoga and Hubberton, where he was severely wounded. He owned a substantial farm property called Pant Howel near Menai Bridge in Anglesey and in 1789 married his first cousin, Jane Vincent, daughter of his uncle, the Reverend James Vincent. Their eldest son was named James Vincent Jones.

James Vincent Jones, born in 1792, like some previous members of his family was educated at Jesus College, Oxford, receiving his M.A. in 1817. He was ordained at Christ Church and was a Fellow of Jesus from 1816, concurrently holding the curacy of Llangadwaladr in southern Anglesey, which was a living in the gift of his college. In 1820, at the age of 28, the Reverend James Vincent Jones changed his name to James V. Vincent. He did this, not from any wish to obscure his father's name, but rather to maintain the existence of the Vincent name which was in danger of dying out through lack of male Vincents in his mother's generation. It also emphasised the fact that he was three-quarters Vincent with his mother and paternal grandmother being respectively granddaughter and daughter of the original Thomas Vincent.

The Reverend James V. Vincent resigned his fellowship at Jesus in 1824 in order to marry. He took up a curacy at the village of Betws Garmon, five miles south-east of Caernarfon in the Snowdonia foothills. He and his new bride, however, chose to live at Llandegfan, on the Anglesey side of the Menai Strait at Pant Howel, the family home where his father, Captain John Jones, had died in the previous year. This would have involved him in considerable travel, which increased in the following year, 1825, when he also became priest-in-charge at Llanfair-is-Gaer, Portdinorwic, between Bangor and Caernarfon. Residing at Llandegfan was at least more convenient for his third concurrent post as curate of Llandegfan with Beaumaris, which he took up in August 1826. James Vincent became rector of Llanfairfechan in 1834, a post which he held for 28 years. He and his wife went to live at Gorddinog, her inheritance, a fine house and estate comprising excellent farmland beneath the coastal foothills some five miles east of Bangor. Gorddinog provided not only a fine, private rectory for his priestly activities, but also enabled James V. Vincent to indulge in two activities which were close to his heart: the breeding of Welsh Black cattle and greyhounds. This did not detract, however, from the quality of his clerical work, which was recognised when he was appointed Second Canon of Bangor Cathedral in 1851. In

James V. Vincent,
Rector of
Llanfairfechan (1834-62)
and Dean of
Bangor (1862-76),
grandfather of the
Vincent children.
(Sir Kyffin Williams)

1862, he became the Dean of Bangor.

James V. Vincent's occupancy of the Deanery was marked by a radical and thorough programme of cathedral restoration. He appointed Sir George Gilbert Scott RA, the leading architect of the day, as his principal advisor. The Dean raised over £20,000 by public subscription, the largest single contribution being £6,165 from Lord Penrhyn. The Dean's appeal enabled the partial reconstruction of the choir, transepts and crossing of the Cathedral, together with the chapter house. An organ chamber was built in the north transept to receive a new organ built by William Hill. The cost of the organ (£900) was met personally by Dean Vincent. Scott's plans and Vincent's leadership gave new dignity to both the interior and exterior of the cathedral. The restoration was subsequently described as the only occasion since the early fourteenth century when work was done on the Cathedral which was by contemporary standards, of the finest quality.

Dean Vincent and his wife had five sons, all of whom died before their father, and three of whom died before their mother. John Vincent (1825-57) served with the Royal Welch Fusiliers in Canada and died in Australia. James Crawley Vincent (1827-69) followed his father into the Church, and was the only son to marry. Edmund Lloyd Vincent (1830-65), who trained as an engineer on the Chester and Holyhead Railway, emigrated to India where he worked on the East India Railway from Calcutta towards Delhi. He also developed a slate quarrying venture at Monghyr in the Ganges valley. He died in Calcutta at the age of 35. Augustus Edward Vincent (1832-59) went to sea, joining the Peninsular and Oriental Steamship Company. He was involved in the transporting of troops to and from the Crimea and saw much of the world before being accidentally drowned in the Woosung River in China, at the age of 27, while serving as second mate on the *Granada*. The youngest son, Corbet Parry Vincent (1840-72), trained as a surveyor and was a promising and inventive engineer. He spent some time in India with his brother Edmund, then returned home in order to gain further experience but also prematurely died at the age of 32.

The Corbet Lineage

It was the custom of the Vincent family to perpetuate the use of ancestral names, both Christian and surnames. This explains the appearance of the names Corbet and Crawley in the nineteenth century. The name Corbet derives from the Corbet family of Morton Corbet in Shropshire and originated with the Corbets of Caus Castle near Welshpool, who participated in the Third Crusade in the late twelfth century. One member of this family, Sir Peter Corbet, at the Battle of Falkirk in 1298, carried arms which included "a corbyn sable" (a black raven). The "corbyn" is a probable allusion to the Danish standard carried by their ancestors under Rollo the Dane, who died in 920, and was the Norseman who conquered Normandy. Another direct ancestor was Sir Robert Corbet of Moreton Corbet, who in 1500, married Elizabeth Vernon, daughter of Sir Henry Vernon and Lady Anne Talbot, daughter of the second Earl of Shrewsbury and his wife, Lady Elizabeth Butler. It is through Lady Elizabeth Butler that the Corbet and Vincent families derive from the royal houses of both England and Spain. She was directly descended from King Edward I by his first marriage, in 1254, to Eleanor of Castile.[3]

Sir Robert and his wife, Elizabeth Vernon, are commemorated by their marble effigies on a magnificent, painted chest-tomb, which can be seen in St Bartholomew's Church at Moreton Corbet. Their grandson, Sir Andrew, built nearby an imposing new manor house. In the next generation came the first Corbet

---

[3] see Appendix 3

4

The ruins of the Elizabethan manor house of Moreton Corbet, the ancestral home of the Corbet family from medieval times. The house, standing alongside the ruins of the medieval castle, was itself never restored following the damage sustained during the Civil War.

baronet called Vincent (1555–1623). His youngest son, Robert Corbet, married Bridget Pryse who was descended from an ancient Welsh family called Wynn holding the rich and fertile estate of Ynys y Maengwyn on the coast near Aberdovey. Their son, named Vincent after his grandfather, inherited his mother's estate. His son, also Vincent (1651–1723), married Anne Vaughan of the ancient house of Corsygedol and together they had three children. The first child, and only son, given, under the Welsh patronymic system, the name Thomas ap Vincent, had been born prior to their marriage. Possibly owing to the illegitimacy of his actual birth, Thomas ap Vincent did not inherit the Ynys y Maengwyn estate of his father, which passed to his sister Anne Corbet. He was, however, provided with a first class education and entered the Church. Thomas dropped the "ap", probably whilst at Trinity College, Cambridge, and therefore, the first cleric in the family, was also the first to bear the surname "Vincent".

Neither Thomas Vincent nor his wife Jane Anwyl inherited any property

Ynys y Maengwyn, birthplace of Vincent Corbet, the father of Rev. Thomas Vincent. The house was demolished after World War II. Traces are still visible. (Gwynedd Archives)

Corsygedol, the ancestral home of Anne Vaughan, mother of Rev. Thomas Vincent.

Parc, the ancestral home of Jane Anwyl, the wife of Rev. Thomas Vincent.

Llugwy, the family home of Jane Anwyl's mother, Joanna Price.

from their respective paternal or maternal families, but their marriage combined the blood lines of four very eminent Welsh families. These were the ancient Houses and estates of the Wynns and Corbets of Ynys y Maengwyn (three and a half miles north of Aberdovey); the Vaughans of Corsygedol (five miles south-east of Harlech); the Anwyls of Parc (four miles south-east of Beddgelert); and the Prices of Llugwy (one mile west of Machynlleth, an ancient seat of Parliament for the Principality of Gwynedd). Remarkably, all four of these houses, three of which still stand, were all situated just within the boundary of the present Snowdonia National Park.

The Crawley Family

It was the marriage between James V. Vincent and Margaret Matilda Crawley in 1824 which linked the families of Vincent and Crawley. Her father, Captain John Crawley RN, and his elder brother Admiral Edward Crawley RN (1750-1834) both retired from Nelson's navy after taking part in the Battle of the Nile. The Admiral commanded *HMS Lion*, a ship of 64 guns on which, at an earlier period, Lord Nelson had himself served under Cornwallis. Captain Crawley had commanded *HMS Leviathan*. It was possibly with bounty money that Captain Crawley bought the house and estate of Gorddinog near the village of Llanfairfechan, with its fine views across the Lavan Sands to Anglesey. For a time he was joined at Gorddinog by his brother.

Edward and John Crawley were the sons of Edmund Crawley of Halifax, Nova Scotia, a member of His Majesty's Council for Nova Scotia, who had been granted 10,000 acres in the vicinity of the harbour of Pictou in Nova Scotia. The Crawley family is traceable through Sir Francis Crawley, Judge of the Court of Common Pleas in 1632, to John Crawley "Lord of the manor of Havering and other lands in Luton, Bedfordshire", who was living in 1550.[4]

The Crawley brothers married two first cousins. Captain Crawley married Margaret Roberts, daughter of the Reverend Griffith Roberts, Rector of Aber, the coastal parish adjacent to Gorddinog. Admiral Crawley married her cousin Elizabeth Jones of Castellmai, Caernarfon. Elizabeth Jones was the heiress to the estate of Treborth Uchaf through her mother, who was the daughter of Lodwig Hughes of Treborth Uchaf (1675-1730).

It was through their Welsh mothers that the children of Admiral Crawley

---

[4] see Appendix 4

inherited Treborth Uchaf and the elder daughter of Captain Crawley inherited Gorddinog. With the marriage of Margaret Matilda Crawley to the Reverend James V. Vincent, Gorddinog came into the Vincent family. Admiral Crawley and his wife eventually settled in Teignmouth and their son, the Venerable Edmund Jones Crawley, Prebendary of Bath and Wells, eventually inherited the Treborth Uchaf estate. It was he who bequeathed Treborth Uchaf to the fatherless grandchildren of his first cousin, Margaret Matilda Vincent, in 1871. Thus through the marriage of two Crawley brothers to two Welsh first cousins, the Vincent family inherited two valuable homes.

2. THE PARENTS OF THE CHILDREN OF TREBORTH

The Reverend James Crawley Vincent (1827-1869)

James Crawley Vincent was born on 23rd April 1827, at his late grandfather's home, Pant Howel, Llandegfan, in Anglesey. He was the second child of the family, his elder brother, John Vincent, having been born two years previously, in 1825. The family remained at the fine Georgian house of Pant Howel, which nestled in well wooded and rolling countryside, until 1834, by which time James had two younger brothers, Edmund and Augustus. When James V. Vincent became the vicar of the mainland parish of Llanfairfechan at the northern end of the Menai Strait, the family left Anglesey.

At the age of eight, James' formal education commenced, and he was sent to the Merchant Taylors' School in London, where he remained from 1835 until 1844. Visiting his parents during school holidays would have entailed an arduous round-trip of 500 miles. Family records show that in 1835 the journey had to be undertaken by mail coach, but the growth of the railway network meant that from 1836 onwards he used the steam packet to get to Liverpool, and from there travelled to London by train. In his final year at the Merchant Taylors', James was the school's Head Prompter, and clearly demonstrated considerable academic ability. He won the Greek Verse Prize, and gained an exhibition, worth £35 a year, to Jesus College, Oxford. In the following year, he received an additional scholarship, open to North Wales students, provided by the Meyrick family of Anglesey. According to Foster's *Alumni Oxonienses*, James Crawley Vincent matriculated on November

The Rev. James Crawley Vincent (1827-69), second son of Dean Vincent and father of the Vincent children. (Sir Kyffin Williams)

28th 1844 and took his B.A. in 1849. In spite of his early promise, he did not graduate with an honours degree, but these were relatively unusual at the time. His sporting activities may well have conflicted with his academic studies. He had been an enthusiastic rower on the Thames when at school, and was a founder member of the Jesus College Boat Club which was established in 1846. The records reveal that J.C. Vincent was its first captain, and his close friend, David Watkin Davies, whose family appears forty years later in the Diary, was the coxswain.

James seems to have left Oxford with the intention of following his father into the Church. It seems likely, however, that both he and his father were of the opinion that his education would be more satisfactorily completed by taking advantage of an opportunity to travel and work abroad. Through a common friend, his father was able to arrange for James to become tutor to the son of a wealthy shipping broker, James Close, living in Naples. Close, also owner of his own merchant line, had strong commercial connections with the court of King Ferdinand of Naples and moved in the affluent and fashionable English community which was then resident in that city. Vincent worked for the Close family from late 1849 until mid 1851. During this period, he travelled widely with James Close, sailing throughout the Mediterranean and Aegean region, and particularly enjoying the opportunity to visit and study many classical Greco-Roman sites. He had an Italian teacher, and also attempted to gain competence in both German and French. Correspondence with his father at this time reveals that ordination into the Anglican Church was often in his mind, with discussion as to whether he should be ordained by the Bishop of Gibraltar, on one of the latter's pastoral visits to Naples. Having spent so much of his life away from Welsh speakers, James feared he might never achieve the bi lingual fluency required by the Anglican Church in Wales. He, therefore, contemplated entering the English Church and expressed a preference for an urban, industrial parish.

James Crawley Vincent, at the age of 24, returned to Britain and attended the Great Exhibition of 1851. On returning to Wales, his mind quickly cleared regarding where he should enter the Church. He rapidly became proficient in Welsh and was ordained as a priest at the Cathedral in Bangor. Between 1852 and 1854, he was curate in the extremely rural parish of Llantrisant in western Anglesey. Here he met his future wife, Grace Elizabeth Johnson, possibly through her brother, the Reverend Hugh Molloy Johnson, the curate of a neighbouring parish and

Llanbeblig Church, Caernarfon, where James Crawley Vincent was vicar from 1859 to 1869.

Vincent's contemporary at Jesus College. For two years, Vincent moved from the Diocese of Bangor to that of St Asaph, where he was curate of Dyserth in Flintshire. He married Grace Johnson on February 6th 1855. Returning to the Bangor Diocese in 1856, Vincent, under the patronage of the future first Baron Penrhyn, became curate at the new church of Glanogwen, and then priest-in-charge at St Anne's, both in the small slate-quarrying town of Bethesda. In 1859 he was appointed vicar of Llanbeblig with Caernarfon, where he quickly established himself as a most popular priest. Shortly after his father became Dean in 1862, the younger James became Rural Dean of Arfon and initiated the building of a strikingly fine new church, Christ Church, in Caernarfon.

James and Grace's first child was born in 1856 but died two days later. The next two children, James Edmund and Mary Matilda, were born in 1857 and 1859 respectively, both at St Anne's, Bethesda. The remaining six children were born at Llanbeblig Vicarage, Caernarfon: Ellen Augusta Crawley (1860); Hugh Corbet (1862); Evangeline Margaret (1863); William Henry Hoare (1866); Grace Georgiana Wynne (1867); and Augustus Edward (1868). When the youngest child was just one year old, James Crawley Vincent died on September 8th 1869,

Caernarfon Vicarage, where six of the Vincent children were born. It was demolished in the 1950s. (Vida Lloyd-Jones)

following a tracheotomy operation and the insertion of a tube in the throat. His health had been failing for some time, following his exertions during the Caernarfon cholera outbreak of 1867, throughout which he tirelessly ministered, not only to his own parishioners, but to all who were in need.

At the time of the cholera epidemic, the Mayor of Caernarfon was Sir Llewelyn Turner, who recorded:

> In my capacity as Mayor and Chairman of the Board of Health, I was associated with the Rev. J.C. Vincent during the cholera pestilence in Carnarvon in the year 1867. Having accompanied Mr Vincent in daylight through all the abominable and disgraceful haunts of misery when the cholera first broke out, nobody could better realise than I, the horror of visits to the dens to which he was summoned at all hours of the night, summonses to which he responded with a readiness that was worthy of all praise. Mr Vincent was a man of fine physique, standing about six feet two, and as brave as a lion. The admirable conduct of Mr Vincent and Mr David Thomas, relieving officer, endeared them to me, and when I followed Mr Vincent to the graveside, I was painfully reminded that the locality was deprived of a man whose services in a great emergency had lightened the departure of a large number of unfortunate people who were carried off by the pestilence…. The respect in which he was held was amply displayed at his funeral, which was attended by a vast concourse of people of all classes.

Grace Elizabeth Vincent née Johnson (1828-1899)

The marriage of James Crawley Vincent and Grace Elizabeth Johnson, on February 6th 1855, linked two clerical families. The ceremony took place at Llanfaethlu, the Anglesey parish church of Grace's father, the Reverend William Johnson. The couple had something of an embarrassment of clergymen who could have performed the ceremony for them: Grace's only surviving siblings were also both clergymen. James' father was rather concerned that his son was marrying at too early a stage in his career, before he had a satisfactory income with which to support a family. In letters to another son, Edmund, then in India, James' mother expressed worries about the delicacy of Grace's health and his father confessed to having serious reservations. However, he recognised their right to marry, happily attended the wedding and wished them every blessing.

Grace was born on August 20th 1828, the third child and first daughter of the Reverend William Johnson (1791-1863) and his wife Ellen, née Wynne-Jones (1796-1834). At the time of her birth, William Johnson was perpetual curate of the parish of Amlwch on the north coast of Anglesey. As such he was the priest in charge of a large parish, which included the then flourishing copper mines of Parys Mountain. Her elder brothers were William and Hugh who were respectively four and two years older than herself. Two sisters, Margaret Jane and Mary Ellen were born in 1830 and 1833.

Tragedy hit the family in 1834 when Ellen Johnson, never having recovered from the birth of her youngest child, died. She was buried in the chancel of her family church at Bodedern, in west central Anglesey. As Ellen was the youngest of nine children of the Wynne-Jones family of the Treiorwerth estate near Bodedern, the bereaved Johnsons were not short of consolation, and there was ready practical help for William Johnson in the upbringing of his children.

Nothing is known of Grace's early education, but at the age of 14 she was already attending Mrs Ayrton's School at Abbot's Grange, near Chester. Her father's very affectionate letters written to her in 1842, reveal deep concerns about her health and clearly suggest that she had already, whilst at the school, suffered some type of debilitating illness. Her father had moved from Amlwch in 1840, to become vicar of Heneglwys, (Gwalchmai, in central Anglesey) where he remained for four years. During this period, Grace's two brothers, the younger William Johnson and Hugh Molloy Johnson proceeded to university. William followed his father to Trinity College, Dublin, and Hugh went to Jesus College, Oxford. At Oxford Hugh became closely associated with James Crawley Vincent, his academic contemporary.

Grace's father moved to the parish of Llanfaethlu, in north-western Anglesey, in 1844. Two years later, when Grace was aged 18, her sister Margaret died of tuberculosis at the age of 15, and within a year, her younger sister, Ellen, died at the age of 14. William Johnson arranged for their burial in the graveyard of his first Anglesey church at Llandrygarn, where his own mother had been buried in 1843. With her brothers at college, Grace became her father's sole consolation. In the next few years, her two brothers left college and both entered the Church. William Johnson, after being the second master at Ruthin School, became vicar of the parish of Llanbadrig with its ancient cliff-top church on the north coast of Anglesey. Hugh Johnson was for a time the curate of Llanfwrog, in his father's parish of Llanfaethlu-with-Llanfwrog.

In 1854, after twenty years as a widower, the Reverend William Johnson senior remarried at the age of 63. His new wife was Sarah Isabella Carmichael of Twickenham, Middlesex, aged 37. It was in the following year that his daughter Grace married James Crawley Vincent. Six months after Grace's wedding, her stepmother gave birth to a son, Frederic William. Two more half brothers, Ernest Carmichael and Edward Arthur, arrived in 1857 and 1858. During the same period, Grace, whose health continued to be of concern, lost her first child, a daughter called Margaret Matilda, after two days, and suffered a miscarriage in the following year.

3. THE MATERNAL FAMILY HISTORY

The Johnson Family

The Johnson family name had a very short and extraordinary history. The Reverend William Johnson (1791-1863) was the first member of his family to carry that surname. He was born in Ireland, the son of Elizabeth Jaques (1767-1843), a member of a respectable Huguenot family living in Dublin. His father was William Magee (1766-1831), a graduate of Trinity College, Dublin, who as a recently appointed fellow of the college, met Elizabeth Jaques while privately tutoring her brother. The history of their relationship was recorded, in 1927, in a commonplace book kept by Mollie Vincent:

> William Magee, who was a fellow of Trinity College (who in those days were not allowed to marry and keep their fellowships) had no other means … fell in love with Elizabeth Jaques. Some form of marriage was gone through which satisfied her. When she found that she was to become a mother, she asked Magee to give up the fellowship and proclaim the marriage. Failing to prevail on her to keep silence, he declared the ceremony of marriage to be illegal. She left him and fled to Llanrwst. [*Why she went to Llanrwst, in the Conwy Valley of North Wales, is unknown*]. She supported herself and the child by teaching French. The father later educated the boy in Ireland, first at school and then at [*Trinity*] College. The mother seems to have removed to Anglesey and kept a small school at Cemaes [*on the north coast of the island*]. The boy lived with his mother in

15

the vacation and learnt to speak in Welsh. After he left college his father got him a tutorship, after which he was ordained … Whether Elizabeth Jaques had or had not been married to William Magee remains a question.

Whatever the truth of the situation, at about the time Elizabeth Jaques left Ireland, William Magee was ordained into the Anglican Church. Apparently mistaking the English usage of Jack (John) as the equivalent of her own family name, Jaques, she gave her son the name Johnson. Magee married – or remarried – in 1793, became Donellan lecturer in 1795, and Professor of Mathematics at Trinity College in 1800. He was then successively Dean of Cork (1813-19), Bishop of Raphoe (1819-22) and Archbishop of Dublin (1822-31).

Elizabeth was living in Anglesey and was joined on the island by her son, William Johnson, when in 1816, he took up his first clerical appointment as curate in the parish which is today centred on the community of Bryngwran, seven miles east of Holyhead. It would appear that he was ordained in Dublin. How he came to the diocese of Bangor is not known with certainty, but it would seem likely that William Magee, then Dean of Cork, exerted some influence out

Archbishop William Magee (1766-1831), grandfather of Grace Vincent and great-grandfather of the Vincent children. Magee was successively Professor of Mathematics at Trinity College, Dublin, Dean of Cork, Bishop of Raphoe and Archbishop of Dublin. (The Authors by permission of TCD)

of consideration for both Elizabeth and their son. William Johnson became perpetual curate of Llandrygarn in 1818. He was now the priest in charge of the parish which straddled the turnpike road across Anglesey and included the Gwyndy Inn, the last staging post on the London to Holyhead road. One of his parishioners was the government postmaster at Gwyndy for the King's Packet to Ireland, Hugh Jones (1752-1821). William Johnson was responsible for the meeting between his mother and Hugh Jones and their marriage took place, probably in 1819, though no record of the ceremony can be found. Hugh Jones died in 1821, and was buried in Llandrygarn churchyard. Elizabeth was appointed postmistress in his stead, but how long she served is not known. What is certain is that the Gwyndy Inn gradually diminished in importance after the construction of Thomas Telford's new turnpike road, which was completed prior to the opening of the Menai Suspension Bridge in 1825. Elizabeth retired to her husband's property of Rhyd Caradog, close to Llandrygarn church, where she was buried with him in 1843. Elizabeth's had not been an easy life. For over 20 years she supported herself as a single parent in a country that was foreign to her. She then enjoyed but a short marriage, followed by 22 years of widowhood. Through this long period she was sustained by her only child, William Johnson.

The Wynne-Joneses of Treiorwerth

When the Reverend William Johnson married his first wife, Ellen Wynne-Jones, in 1823 at Bodedern, the neighbouring parish to Llandrygarn, he joined a family which had particularly deep roots in Anglesey.[5] Ellen's father, the Reverend Hugh Wynne-Jones (1751-1809), had been High Sheriff of Anglesey in 1773 at the unusually young age of 22. He rebuilt the house of Treiorwerth, where he and his wife brought up their large family. Ellen's mother, Grace Williams (1754-1816), was yet another daughter of the Church, her father being the Reverend Robert Williams, rector of Llanystumdwy near Criccieth.

The nine Wynne-Jones children were born over a 20-year period. The eldest, named after his father Hugh, was born in 1776 and Ellen, the youngest, was born in 1796 when her mother was aged 42. Hugh followed his father into the Church and, like him, was successively perpetual curate of Bodedern (1811) and

---

[5] see Appendix 5

rector of Llantrisant (1820), also serving as Chancellor of Bangor Cathedral from 1818 to his death in 1849. Of Ellen's remaining four brothers, one, Robert became a surgeon, and another, William, a Royal Naval captain.

The second Hugh Wynne-Jones inherited Treiorwerth and had eight children. This generation of the Wynne-Jones family – six boys and two girls – were the first cousins of Grace Johnson, but were a good deal older. Of these cousins, three of the boys entered the Church, one became a surgeon in Beaumaris, the then county town of Anglesey, and another was a captain in the East India Company. The most prominent locally and in Grace's adult life, was the Reverend John Wynne-Jones (1804-1888), who became Archdeacon of Bangor in 1863 and retained that office for 24 years. The Venerable John Wynne-Jones had a residence in Bangor only two miles from Grace and her children at Treborth Uchaf. He also inherited the Treiorwerth estate and was the owner in the 1880s, when the Family Diary shows that the Vincent family members made frequent visits.

Treiorwerth, the Wynne-Jones family home near Bodedern, Anglesey.

Part Two: The Vincents and their Social Circle

4. THE VINCENT CHILDREN IN 1885

At the beginning of 1885 when the Vincent Diary commences, Grace and all her children, with the exception of Ted, are resident at Treborth or regularly returning home during vacations. Ted had graduated from Christ Church, Oxford, in 1880, and taken a teaching post at a school in Elstree, Hertfordshire, but one term had been sufficient to make him realise that he had made the wrong career choice. He entered the Inner Temple in 1881 and supported himself by tutoring the sons of Judge Watkin Wynn at their home in Pimlico. In 1884 he was called to the Bar and got married. His new wife, Mary Alexandra Cook – known within the family as Babs – was the daughter of Silas Kemball Cook, who was the Governor of the Seaman's Hospital at Greenwich. Ted had just begun to practise on the North Western and North Wales Circuit. He also acted as a reporter for the *Law Times* and seems to have been already finding journalism more attractive than the law. In this and his future career, Ted may well have been influenced by his brother-in-law, Edward Cook. The latter had been his close friend at both Winchester and Oxford, where he had been a greatly admired President of the Union, and was now gaining a reputation as a journalist. Sir Edward Cook, as he became, was successively editor of *The Pall Mall Gazette, The Westminster Gazette,* and *The Daily News.* Not only was Cook undoubtedly the means of Ted meeting his wife, but in 1880 he had come close to entering the Vincent family when he was engaged briefly to Mollie Vincent.

Hugh, after leaving Sherborne, had completed an arts degree at Trinity College, Dublin. As a Welshman studying in Ireland, Hugh had found himself in the highly unusual position of being offered an international rugby cap by both nations when they met in June 1882. Hugh chose to play for the Welsh team, which went on to win the match. He subsequently studied for and sat his law examinations in London and was initially articled to the company of Charles A. Jones in Caernarfon. Hugh Vincent also had a strong interest in association football, and whilst serving his articles, he played centre-half for Carnarvon Wanderers. During this period, which is covered by the Family Diary, he began to appear in court regularly on behalf of his company's clients.

James Edmund 'Ted'

Hugh Corbet

William Henry Hoare

Augustus Edward 'Gustie'

The third son, William, was aged 19 in 1885. He had been educated at Friars' School, which was at the time still situated on the site of its foundation, the former Dominican friary in the lower part of the city of Bangor. The headmaster was the Reverend Dr Daniel Lewis Lloyd who was undoubtedly a considerable influence upon William's formative years. Dr Lloyd greatly enhanced the scholastic reputation of the historic grammar school. He also introduced both cricket and association football into its sporting activities. William developed a love of cricket, which remained with him for life. When Daniel Lewis Lloyd left Bangor in September 1879 to become headmaster at Christ College, Brecon, the 14 year-old William was one of several boys who went with him. It was whilst he was at Brecon that William became interested in a career in the Indian Civil Service (ICS). It is not known how this came about, whether by peer influence or otherwise. He left Brecon in July 1883 at the age of 17. When the Diary starts in 1885, William is in London, nearing completion of two years' preparation for the ICS entry examinations at a school established for that purpose at Powis Square, Notting Hill. During 1885 he passed the examinations and the Diary shows that his subsequent training is split between Trinity College, Dublin and London.

The youngest son, Gustie, was aged 16 at the beginning of 1885, and had left Friars' School in the summer of the previous year. He then spent part of the year 1884 studying in France at the Ecole Saint Elme, at Arcachon near Bordeaux, before entering the new University College of North Wales at Bangor to study French, Mathematics and Greek in January 1885. Gustie's objective seems to have been to prepare himself for officer entry into the army.

The two youngest Vincent daughters, Eva and Georgie, aged 20 and 17, had enrolled at the new college in the previous November. They and a number of their friends were part of the very first intake of students in the college's foundation year. Eva was registered as student number 50 and Georgie as number 52. Their elder sisters, Mollie aged 25, and Lil aged 24, also entered the college at the beginning of its second term in January 1885. Surviving course enrolment cards show that Mollie, Lil and Georgie all followed courses in English History and Literature. Of all the girls, Georgie was the only one who followed a prolonged course of study. Eva was not enjoying good health and the fact that the Diary does not mention her attendance at lectures, suggests she had already been forced to withdraw from her studies. Mollie, the legal owner of the property, was largely helping her mother to run the family home at Treborth and did not continue her studies beyond two terms. Lil, already engaged, was due to marry in the summer of 1885, and therefore her

Mary Matilda 'Mollie'

Ellen Augusta Crawley 'Lil'

Evangeline Margaret 'Eva'

Grace Georgiana Wynne 'Georgie'

college plans were only short term. Her future husband, John Jordan Lloyd-Williams – Jack – who is staying with the Vincent family when the Diary commences, had first met Lil when he came to Bangor from his home in Cardiganshire to attend Friars' School, where his uncle, Daniel Lewis Lloyd, was the headmaster. Daniel Lewis Lloyd, a future Bishop of Bangor, was, therefore, not only a close friend of the Vincent family, but also had a profound influence upon the lives of two of the Vincent children.

5. THE VINCENT FAMILY FRIENDS

Their Cousins: the Johnsons and Wynne-Joneses

James Crawley Vincent was predeceased by three of his four brothers, none of whom had married. The only cousins of the children of Treborth were therefore on their mother's side of the family.[6]

Grace Vincent's elder brother, the younger Reverend William Johnson, after being vicar of Llanbadrig, was rector of Llaniestyn on the Llŷn Peninsula for 22 years and was still there during the period of the Diary. He had also become First Canon of Bangor in 1868 and this required frequent visits to Bangor and the cathedral. This William Johnson had married his second cousin, Emma Pilkington Walker, daughter of the eminent Irish barrister, Richard Cotton Walker KC, frequently referred to as "the Father of the Irish Bar". They had 11 children, who were first cousins to the children of James Crawley Vincent and his wife Grace.

Eight of the children survived into adulthood. Not one of the five sons followed the family tradition of entering the Church. The eldest, Hugh Johnson (born 1858), did get as far as being ordained, but must have caused some consternation in both his family and the Church when he converted to Islam. An Oxford-educated linguist and philologist, he became a professor at the University of Cairo. Trevor Griffith Johnson M.A., was head boy of Malvern and was the highest placed student of his graduating class at Trinity College, Dublin, where he won three gold medals in classics, before proceeding to Cambridge and earning two more gold medals. A potentially glittering career was tragically cut short by

---

[6] see Appendix 5

early blindness. Two of the brothers became solicitors: Edward William Johnson (1866-1917) was a founder of Chamberlain, Johnson and Park, solicitors of Llandudno, where he was later joined by his younger brother Richard Vincent Johnson (1872-1951), who like his cousin Hugh Vincent, played rugby for Wales. The remaining brother, James Campbell Johnson (1868-1887), who was close to William Vincent, died at the age of 19.

Of the three daughters, the eldest, Margaret Wynne Johnson (1861-1933) was a life-long friend of Mollie Vincent, and it was she who was the source of Mollie's account of their common great-grandfather, William Magee. Her two sisters were Frances Ellen Johnson (born 1867) who is known to have married, and Emma Marland Johnson (born 1870) who died in 1893 at the age of 23.

In addition, there were the three children resulting from the second marriage of Grace Vincent's father, the first William Johnson. They were Frederic, Ernest and Edward, born in 1855, 1857 and 1858 respectively. Although uncles to the Vincents of Treborth, these three Johnsons were very much of an age with their nephews and nieces. Fred Johnson who stays at Treborth Uchaf and also pays a visit to his half brother at the Llaniestyn rectory, is the only member of this branch of the family to appear in the Diary.

The Vincent children also saw a great deal of their second cousins, who were the children of Grace Vincent's cousin, the Venerable John Wynne-Jones, the Archdeacon of Bangor. There were five of these second cousins, three boys and two girls. The eldest boy, Hugh, emigrated to North America and died in New York in 1898. The second boy, J.W. (Will) Wynne-Jones (1849-1928) followed his father into the Church. He was educated at Eton and Christ Church before becoming vicar of Aberdare, where he married the second daughter of Lord Aberdare in 1878. In the first year covered by the Diary, he became vicar of Caernarfon, the post formerly held by James Crawley Vincent. He was a regular visitor to the Vincent home. His younger brother, Robert Wynne-Jones, appears in the Diary as comptroller of the Anglesey Hunt and is referred to in accounts of the hunt ball. He had gone to the University of Edinburgh intending to read medicine, but transferred to a biochemistry course for which he received sponsorship from the Younger brewing family. He entered the brewing industry at the Alloa brewery, then became head brewer at the Younger brewery at Holyrood, Edinburgh and was later a director of the Greenall Company at Warrington. His medical connections in Edinburgh, however, provided the link which led to one of the two sisters, Mary Wynne-Jones, marrying Joseph Cotterill, who became an eminent Edinburgh

The Rev. Will Wynne-Jones, who was vicar of Caernarfon from 1885 to 1920. He is pictured (seated second right) in his additional role as chaplain of Caernarfon Gaol. (Gwynedd Archives)

Robert and Meg Wynne-Jones (University of Wales, Bangor)

surgeon. Mary was a close friend of Mollie Vincent, as was her sister Georgina Margaret (Meg), who did not marry, and lived for many years with her father, the Archdeacon, in Bangor. Of her it was said, "she would have spilt her blood for the Church of England, which she loved".

Despite the long clerical heritage shared by the Vincent, Johnson and Wynne-Jones families, of the 12 male cousins and second cousins only one, the Reverend Will Wynne-Jones, entered the Church. In its choice of professions, this was the generation which made a break with the past.

The Ramsays of Beaumaris and London

The Diary contains numerous references to the Ramsays. The family comprised Andrew, Louisa, and their children, Ella, Fanny, Dora, Violet, and Allan. The Ramsays maintained a house, 7 Victoria Terrace, in Beaumaris, Anglesey, where they spent holidays, but their permanent home was in London. They lived initially at 29 Upper Phillimore Place, Kensington, and later moved to 15 Cromwell Crescent in Earl's Court, where the Vincents paid visits at the time of the Diary. Louisa (1825-1917) was born Mary Louisa Williams, daughter of the Reverend James Williams, who was Chancellor of Bangor Cathedral from 1851 until his death in 1872. He was the first cousin of Dean James V. Vincent of Bangor, their mothers, Eleanor and Jane Vincent, being sisters.[7] Coincidentally, James Vincent and James Williams were also, for at least six years, contemporaries as Fellows at Jesus College, Oxford, prior to their both returning to North Wales.

Louisa was therefore a second cousin of James Crawley Vincent, and their correspondence reveals that they were extremely close friends until the latter's death. He was godfather to her only son Allan, and to his children she was 'Aunt Louisa'. Louisa met her future husband, a Scotsman, Andrew Ramsay when he was an officer of the Geological Survey of Great Britain, working in Anglesey. The introduction came through Charles Darwin, whose family, living at The Mount in Shrewsbury, were next-door neighbours to the family of Louisa's mother. Ramsay stayed over the Christmas and New Year period of 1850-51 at the rectory of Llanfairynghornwy in north-western Anglesey, where Louisa's father was the rector.

Andrew Crombie Ramsay (1817-1891) was a scientist of prodigious talent. He had left school at the age of 13 and worked in an office in Glasgow before

---

[7] see Appendix 1

Sir Andrew and Lady Louisa Ramsay (Sir Kyffin Williams)

joining the Geological Survey as a prospective field geologist at the age of 24 in 1841. His geological mapping throughout Anglesey and Snowdonia, much of it carried out on horseback, and using the only available, one inch to the mile scale Ordnance Survey maps, was of an extraordinarily high standard. He was the first geologist truly to appreciate the geological structure of North Wales and also to recognise the modifying effects of glaciation upon the topography of the region. When, in 1849, Ramsay delivered a discourse at the Royal Institution on *The Geological Phenomena that have produced or modified the Scenery of North Wales,* not only was it rapturously received, but Michael Faraday went up to him at the close, shook him by both hands and asked in admiration, "Where did you learn to lecture?" It was perhaps not surprising that in May, 1851, when the Prince Consort opened the new Museum of Practical Geology, off Piccadilly, Andrew Ramsay became the first Professor of Geology in the Royal School of Mines, which together with the Geological Survey, was housed within the museum. A year later, he married the 27 year-old Louisa Williams. The ceremony, in July 1852, was performed by the Reverend James V. Vincent and witnessed by his son, James Crawley Vincent, just a few days prior to his own ordination.

Andrew Ramsay's masterwork was *The Geology of North Wales*, first published in 1866 as Memoir Three of the Geological Survey of Great Britain. In 1872, Ramsay succeeded Sir Roderick Murchison as Director-General of the Geological Survey. As Director, Ramsay introduced more detailed mapping on the larger scale of six inches to the mile. He was essentially responsible for setting the highest modern standards of field geology. In 1879 Ramsay was awarded the Royal Medal of the Royal Society. He was knighted on his retirement in 1881. In a semi-official history of the Geological Survey, a more recent Director General, Sir Edward Bailey, refers to "the oft repeated description of Ramsay as the best field geologist in Europe" He had a scintillating career, and from his home on the sea front at Beaumaris he could view the mountains he knew so well.

The Sackville-Wests of Lime Grove

The friends who appear most frequently in the Diary are the various members of the Sackville-West family, of Lime Grove, Port Penrhyn, Bangor. The family comprised father, three sons and two daughters. Lt-Col. The Hon. William Edward Sackville-West had come to North Wales as estate agent and manager to Lord Penrhyn, who lived in his striking neo-Norman Castle on the outskirts of the city, and was owner of the great Penrhyn slate quarries some five miles away at Bethesda, on the edge of Snowdonia. Apart from his duties to Lord Penrhyn, Colonel Sackville-West was a magistrate and county councillor and played a prominent role in local education, taking a particular interest in the many schools on the Penrhyn estate.

William Edward Sackville-West had been born in 1830 at Bourn Hall in Cambridgeshire. He was the sixth son of George West, the fifth Earl de la Warr, and Lady Elizabeth Sackville, heiress to the fourth Duke of Dorset. The couple took the surname Sackville-West by royal licence in 1843. One of their daughters became the second wife of the second Marquess of Salisbury and stepmother to Robert Gascoyne-Cecil, the third Marquess of Salisbury, who became leader of the Conservative Party. Interestingly, therefore, W.E. Sackville-West living quietly in North Wales, had a step-nephew of exactly his own age, who during the politically turbulent period that coincided with the Vincent Diary, twice defeated Gladstone to become Prime Minister.

Educated at Oxford, William Sackville-West had served with the Grenadier Guards during the Crimean War, and in 1860 he married Georgina,

Lt. Col. the Hon. W.E. Sackville-West and his sons Lionel, Charles and Bertrand

Cecilie and Mary Sackville-West (University of Wales, Bangor)

youngest daughter of George Dodwell of Co. Sligo, Ireland. She died in 1883, and their elder daughter, Mary, assumed the role of family hostess at Lime Grove.

Mary and her sister, Cecilie Sackville-West were, at the time of the Diary, very close friends of the Vincent girls, with whom they shared musical tastes and abilities.

Cecilie, Mary and Lionel were in the group of Vincent friends who registered as students together at the University College of Bangor in 1884-5. The other common interests between the families were tennis, the well-being of the Conservative Party, and the life of the Cathedral.

The Sackville-West sons were Lionel, Charles and Bertrand. Lionel (1867-1928) was a particular friend of Will Vincent, one year his elder, with whom he enjoyed various sporting activities. He followed his father to Oxford and succeeded his uncle as third Baron Sackville in 1908, his father having died three years previously. As Baron Sackville, Lionel inherited the immense Tudor mansion of Knole, situated in a thousand acres of parkland and gardens near Sevenoaks in Kent. The house had been given by Queen Elizabeth I to Thomas Sackville, whose descendants have lived there ever since. In 1890 Lionel had married his cousin, the illegitimate daughter of the second Baron Sackville. Lionel had only one child, the writer Victoria Mary (Vita) Sackville-West. The second son, Charles (1870-1962) who appears in the Diary as a boy of 15, followed a military career, and with the rank of Major-General commanded the King's Royal Rifle Corps. The youngest brother, Bertrand, was, like Lionel, educated at Oxford and became a lieutenant-commander in the Royal Navy. All three sons of William Sackville-West served in and survived the First World War. Indeed, Sir Charles Sackville-West KBE, CB, CMG, who succeeded Lionel to become fourth Baron Sackville, was the British representative of the Supreme War Council at Versailles in 1918.

When Colonel Sackville-West left the Penrhyn estate in 1898, an illuminated address from the estate tenants testified to his "special knowledge of the needs of the countryside" and the manner in which his "influence was constantly exerted in favour of the tenant". The Bishop of St Asaph also remarked that "it has never been my lot to know a man who has been more ready to work for the good of others than Colonel West, and it has all been done in the quietest and most unobtrusive manner".

The Davieses of Treborth Hall

The Davies family were the closest neighbours of the Vincents, the Treborth Uchaf estate adjoining the grounds of Treborth Hall. The houses were separated by only two fields and this proximity fostered the lasting friendship between the children of both families. Unlike many of the Vincent friends, the Davieses were Non-conformists rather than Anglicans and Liberal in their politics. Also unlike the Vincents, the Davieses were exceedingly rich. Treborth Hall supported a domestic staff of a dozen with additional gardeners and coaching staff. By contrast, the Vincents employed only a housemaid and a dairymaid who lived in, and one man who acted as both a groom and outdoor servant, who lived in a nearby cottage.

The Davies roots were in central Anglesey. Richard Davies (1778-1849) of Llangefni married Anne Jones (1785-1856) of Coed Howel, Llangristiolus. They had three sons and three daughters. From the modest grocery and provisioning business founded by their father, the three sons, John (1808), Robert (1816) and Richard (1818), developed a large business as timber merchants, iron founders and ship owners. By the time of the death of John, the eldest son, in 1848, the Davies

The Davies family home, Treborth Hall. (John Cowell)

31

Richard Davies, M.P. for Anglesey, and his wife, Annie.

family possessed a fleet of 12 ships, the largest being just over 1,000 tons. Under Robert and Richard Davies and two cousins, the business greatly prospered and the fleet expanded. Robert Davies lived at Bodlondeb, Bangor, looking out over the Menai Strait to the family's business premises on the waterfront in Menai Bridge town. Richard built Treborth Hall, approximately one mile away along the Strait.

In the 20 years up to 1863, the Davies family acquired 37 wooden sailing ships, all of which were built in Quebec, Nova Scotia, or New Brunswick. Their main business in the earlier days was in carrying slate and emigrants to the United States and timber back from Canada. Later vessels were mostly iron-hulled and British-built and included seven ships built by Royden of Liverpool in the three years 1875-77. These were the 'Welsh County' vessels: the *Anglesey, Merioneth, Denbighshire, Flintshire, Carnarvonshire, Cardiganshire* and *Montgomeryshire,* which ranged from 1227 to 1452 tons in weight. The business was gradually dominated by the shipping of coal from Swansea and Cardiff to San Francisco and returning with Californian grain or the lucrative cargo of South American guano. The Davies shipping fleet sailed all the world's oceans.

John

Mary

Katie

Henry

Edith

Enid

Lloyd

Trixie

Arthur

Richard Davies (1818-1896), married Anne Rees (1836-1918), daughter of Henry Rees, an eminent Welsh Calvinistic Methodist minister in Liverpool. Between 1856 and 1877 they had nine children: four sons and five daughters. Richard Davies was High Sheriff of Anglesey in 1858, and in 1868 he was elected the first Nonconformist Member of Parliament for Anglesey. He served as Lord Lieutenant of the County from 1884 until the year of his death, 1896. When the Vincent Diary was written, Richard Davies was, therefore, a man of considerable local consequence, but in 1886, after eighteen years as an M.P., he resigned from parliament in disagreement with Gladstone's proposals for Irish Home Rule. Both Richard Davies and his younger brother, Robert, were noted for their generous philanthropy, in particular to the Calvinistic Methodist Church and its overseas missions.

The eldest child of Richard and Anne Davies, John Robert Davies MA, JP, DL, CBE, succeeded to the management of the family businesses and built a fine house nestling close to the Menai Suspension Bridge on the Bangor shore between Treborth Hall and his uncle Robert's house. John Davies is mentioned in the Diary as a visitor to Treborth Uchaf and it is evident from the Diary that the Vincents took great delight and interest in the two youngest of Richard Davies' children, Beatrice (Trixie) and Arthur. It is, however, the four older Davies daughters, Mary, Katie, Edith and Enid who were exact contemporaries of the four Vincent girls, Mollie, Lil, Eva and Georgie. The girls of both families were constantly visiting each other's homes and maintained life-long friendships, particularly the two eldest daughters, Mollie Vincent and Mary Davies, who remained unmarried.

The Rathbones of Glan-y-Menai

Living in their house in a particularly beautiful situation on the Anglesey shore of the Menai Strait just outside the town of Menai Bridge, the Rathbones were the Welsh branch of the eminent family of Liverpool merchants and philanthropists. The father, Richard Reynolds Rathbone (1820-1898), was the grandson of William Rathbone (1757-1809) who played a leading role in the cause for the abolition of slavery. This William Rathbone was the fourth in an unbroken line of eldest sons called William stretching from 1669 to the present day. Richard Reynolds Rathbone and his wife, Frances Roberts, had three children: Hugh (1862), Mary Frances (1863), and Richard (1864). Father and eldest son were both closely involved with the family company, William Rathbone & Son, Liverpool, which was founded in 1730. The father had been responsible for the company's cotton interests in Egypt and the Sudan, where he lived for several years. In North Wales, Richard Rathbone lived in partial retirement, enjoying his extensive library and his work as a governor of several educational establishments, including the Bangor Normal College. He was particularly close to his first cousin, the sixth William Rathbone, who was perhaps the most conspicuous member of this remarkable family. William Rathbone (1819-1902), one of the principal founders of the Liverpool Royal Infirmary, was Member of Parliament for Liverpool from 1868-1880, then for Carnarvonshire from 1881 to 1895. He spent much of his time with his cousin's family at Glan-y-Menai in Menai Bridge, as did his daughter, Eleanor Rathbone, who herself later became a distinguished Member of Parliament, sitting for the Combined Universities seat between 1929 and 1945. It was she who introduced into parliament the bill providing for family allowances with the stipulation that payment should go to mothers.

Of the Rathbone children, it was Mary Rathbone who was a good friend of Hugh, Eva and Georgie Vincent. The three girls enrolled together for the first term of the new college in the autumn of 1884. Additionally, Mr and Mrs Rathbone exchanged visits with Grace Vincent. Mary Rathbone spent all her life in the Bangor area; she was a member of the University College Council and its vice-president. She was awarded the LL.D degree in recognition of her work throughout Wales in the field of adult education. Like Mollie Vincent, she never married, and the two remained friends until Mary's death in 1937.

Other Social Connections

Not surprisingly, given their clerical family background, many of the friendships made by the younger generation of Vincents were with the children of other such families. Allied to this, a most influential factor was the strong and traditional Welsh association with the University of Oxford, and particularly with Jesus College, where so many of the Welsh clergy were educated. North Wales had a low density of population, but a very high proportion of its vicarages were occupied by Jesus men. All this gave an important element of cohesion to the society of which the Vincents were a part.

One such connection was with the Watkin-Davies family of Llanrhyddlad in north-western Anglesey. The Reverend David Watkin-Davies was priest of this parish between the years 1874 and 1889. He and his wife had four daughters, Mary, Eleanor, Catherine and Dora, and a son, Francis, who attended Worcester Cathedral Choir School with Hugh Vincent. The parents were friends of Grace Vincent and Francis (Frank), Mary and Dora appear several times in the Diary, exchanging visits with the Vincent children. During the period of the Diary, Frank Watkin-Davies, having graduated from Magdalen College, Oxford, became his father's curate at Llanrhyddlad. The Reverend David Watkin-Davies himself, was an exact contemporary of James Crawley Vincent at Jesus College, Oxford, between 1845 and 1849, and he was witness to James and Grace's marriage in 1855. This friendship was further strengthened by proximity when Watkin-Davies became the vicar of Llanfairpwll in 1866, and the two men, now with young families, were the incumbents of parishes just a few miles apart on opposite banks of the Menai Strait. When James Crawley Vincent died three years later, the Watkin-Davieses would have been a considerable support to his widow and young family.

William Vincent's closest friend at the time of the Diary is Harry Griffith of Pentraeth, Anglesey, whose father, the Reverend Joseph William Griffith, was a Jesus College contemporary of Will's father and David Watkin-Davies. Another college connection was the Reverend John Pryce, who married Grace Vincent's cousin and was invited to be Ted Vincent's godfather. He was vicar of Bangor when James Crawley Vincent was vicar of Caernarfon. During the period of the Diary Canon Pryce was living at the Bangor Canonry and subsequently became Archdeacon and later, Dean of Bangor. The Vincents were very frequent visitors to the Canonry, both for lunch after attending the Cathedral and at other times. Mollie Vincent was particularly friendly with Mary, the eldest of the four Pryce daughters.

Mary Pryce regularly organised theatrical readings and musical evenings at the Canonry. At one such evening on March 10th 1885, Mollie and Lil Vincent and a large number of their friends contributed to the programme. Lionel Sackville-West, an accomplished violinist, provided a solo version of the Schubert Funeral March, and his sister Mary gave an interpretation of the adagio of Beethoven's C Major Piano Sonata. Three of the Pryce sisters played Handel's Pastoral Symphony from *The Messiah* as a violin trio, and Mary Pryce gave two violin solos. Katie Davies of Treborth Hall provided two items, Mollie and Lil Vincent sang the Gounod 'Ave Maria' and Mollie sang Mendelssohn's 'O Rest in the Lord'.

In addition to these occasional gatherings, each winter saw regular meetings of what the participants called the Amateur Music Society. This met at the Lime Grove home of the Sackville-Wests at intervals of three weeks. Items were carefully practised and programmes comprised the works of two, or at most three, composers. Mary Sackville-West fulfilled the role of honorary secretary. It would appear that the society functioned largely for the entertainment of the participants, but they and others amongst their friends also provided public concerts for charitable causes, particularly the support of national schools in the Bangor district.

One of the Vincents' musical friends, the Reverend David Ffrangcon-Davies, was destined for international fame as a baritone. The Diary records that on his visits to the family he always sang for them, and in April 1886 the Vincents went to the Bangor Rink to hear him sing the part of Elijah in the oratorio by Mendelssohn. This was the part with which he was particularly identified throughout his later professional career. He was born in Bethesda, the son of a Penrhyn quarryman, and added Ffrangcon to his name when he left Wales for the first time, to study at Oxford. He was ordained a priest in 1884, and at the period of the Diary, he was the curate at Conwy. In 1887 he was encouraged to apply for a vacant minor canonry in the cathedral. This would have made it easier for him to continue his studies with the organist, Dr Roland Rogers, and to become more involved in all aspects of music in the cathedral. The post, however, was given to someone else. He resigned from the Bangor Diocese and took a curacy in the East End of London. Here he had formal singing lessons, and in 1890 he left the Church to become a professional singer. He was enormously successful, particularly in Britain, America and Germany. He became a close friend of Sir Edward Elgar, and sang in the first performances of *The Dream of Gerontius* and *The Apostles*, in which he sang the part of Christ. So punishing, however, was his workload, that it led to a mental breakdown and he spent the last ten years of his life in a mental hospital.

Also a part of amateur music in Bangor during the mid-1880s were Sir Charles and Lady Isham and their three daughters, Louisa, Emily and Isabel, who had a home called Cartrefle just outside the town of Menai Bridge, overlooking the ancient island church of St Tysilio. Sir Charles and Lady Isham played wind instruments and frequently exchanged visits with Grace Vincent. Sir Charles was the tenth baronet and the main family home was Lamport Hall in Northamptonshire. They were an interesting family with many clerics and architects amongst their number, which also included a master of Pembroke College, Oxford, and a rector of Lincoln College, Oxford.

The musical activities were largely the domain of the Vincent girls. Apart from their interest in the team games of football and cricket, the boys' other sports were hunting and shooting, the latter usually being undertaken on their own estate land at Treborth. Hugh and William Vincent were particularly involved in hunting with the Marquess of Anglesey and his Gascogne hounds. The gentlemen ran and the ladies rode; the quarry was the hare and the whole endeavour provided vigorous exercise.

The shared sport of all the Vincents and many of their friends was tennis. The game was enjoying an explosion of popularity at this time, not least because young men and women could play it together. The Wimbledon Championships had been introduced in 1876, and the women's competition had been introduced in 1884. Each summer, four families had tennis days at their homes: the Vincents, Sackville-Wests, Barbers and Wyatts. At Treborth, it was Hugh Vincent who took it on himself carefully to maintain and mark out the grass court, but there was an even finer court on the front lawn of Lime Grove. The Barber family had been very close neighbours of the Vincents following their move into Bangor in 1870. There were six children of a similar age to the Vincents: Alice, Annie, Walter, Frank, Tom and Alfred. The father, Henry Barber, was a solicitor of note at Wellfield in Bangor. He, in fact, may well have been an influence in the decision of both Edmund and Hugh Vincent to enter the law. In later years, the Barber legal practice was bought by Hugh Vincent. By the period of the Diary, Mr Barber is a widower with several of his children still living at home. The family regularly worshipped alongside the Vincents at Bangor Cathedral. The fourth tennis family were the Wyatts who lived at Tan-y-Bryn, a large Penrhyn estate house which stood on the post-road at the entrance to the city of Bangor, close to both Port Penrhyn and the former coaching inn, the Penrhyn Arms. The father, Arthur Wyatt, was a successful and respected manager and agent for Lord Penrhyn's slate quarries at Bethesda. He was also responsible for the running of the fine harbour at Port Penrhyn and the fleet of boats which exported slate to many parts of the world at that time. He also served as a local magistrate. There was a son, Norris and two daughters, Mary and her sister, Margaret Louisa, who was a particularly keen tennis player.

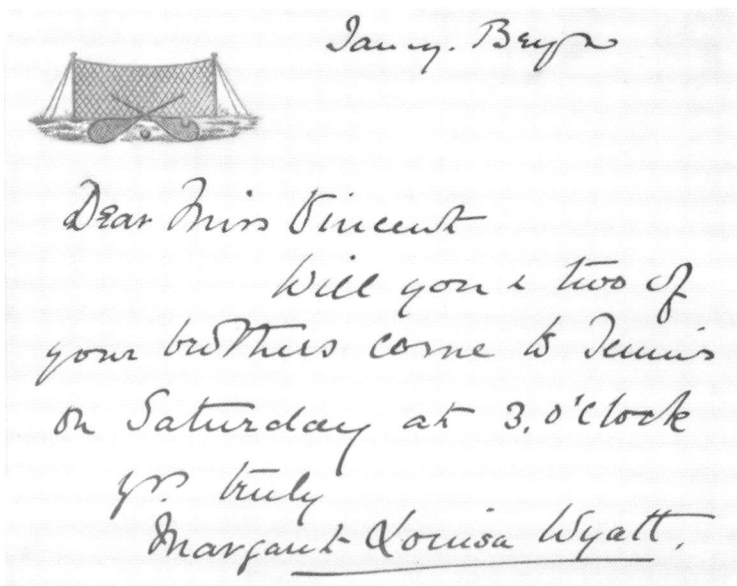

Tan-y. Bryn

Dear Miss Vincent
Will you & two of your brothers come to Tennis on Saturday at 3, o'Clock
yr truly
Margaret Louisa Wyatt,

During the winter months the four families continued to play hard-court tennis at the Bangor Skating Rink, an outdoor facility available for tennis when skating was not feasible. Tennis was arranged on a weekly rota, which in 1885 extended from January 24th to April 18th, each family taking it in turn to hire the courts, provide refreshments and generally act as hosts. The Rink was situated in the valley in which nestled the lower and older part of the city. The facility was owned by a Mr John Stacey and included a drill room, which was also available for hire.

The Vincent Diary reveals that Bangor 'Society' in the late Victorian period already had a closely-knit Anglo-Welsh character, which had been largely brought about by the arrival of the railway in 1850. This had led to an influx of professional men, including architects and engineers, many master craftsmen, printers and publishers, painters and 'photographic artists', together with successful merchants from north-west England, retired military officers and landed gentry. They were drawn by the great natural beauty of the area, and for many there were the added attractions of mountaineering and the opportunities afforded by the Menai Strait for the increasingly fashionable pastime of sailing, which quickly became a symbol of Victorian prosperity.

The popularity of the sport was already established on the Straits, an annual regatta for both yachts and rowing boats having been established at Beaumaris at the beginning of the 1830s and a little later at Caernarfon. Their success prompted the 22 year-old future mayor of Caernarfon, Llewelyn Turner, to organise a club for yachting enthusiasts. This was established as the Royal Welsh Yacht Club in 1847. Henry William Paget, the first Marquis of Anglesey, was the Commodore with Robert Stephenson, who was just completing the Chester and Holyhead Railway, as Vice-Commodore, and Llewelyn Turner himself as Rear-Commodore.

It was in the first year of the Diary, 1885, that the long-established Beaumaris Book Society transformed itself into a yacht club. On the 18th of June of that year the Marquis of Anglesey received a letter stating that "Her Majesty had been graciously pleased to accede to your request and to command that the Anglesey Yacht Club should be styled the Royal Anglesey Yacht Club".

In the mid-1880s, it was again the railway that provided the motive power for a major development which would add a further intellectual dimension to the life of Bangor.

Part 3 : The Local and National Context

6. THE NEW UNIVERSITY COLLEGE OF NORTH WALES

The opening of a university or university college in a provincial town within England or Wales during the Victorian period would have had a quite dramatic influence upon the cultural and social life of the community. The smaller the community, the greater was that effect. Prior to 1880, there were only two institutions with degree-conferring status in Wales. St David's College, Lampeter, established in 1822, was a Church of England foundation, which had been conferring its own B.D. and B.A. degrees from 1852 and 1865 respectively. It had close connections with the universities of Oxford and Cambridge, and provided a good liberal education for men, most of whom were hoping to enter holy orders in the Welsh Church. In North Wales, the Bangor Normal College had been founded in 1847 as a Nonconformist institution. The college offered the opportunity for students to matriculate and sit for degrees conferred by the University of London, but for the most part it trained teachers for the elementary schools of Wales, which had greatly increased in number between 1845 and 1860, largely due to the influence of the Cambrian Educational Society led by Sir Hugh Owen, the greatest of many eminent Welsh educationalists. Apart from St David's College, Bangor Normal College, and a small number of endowed grammar schools, Wales was very poorly provided with either post-elementary or higher education.

Throughout the 1870s and 1880s the movement to improve secondary and higher education in Wales gained momentum. Aberystwyth College was founded in 1872 but, without any government financing, it was almost entirely dependent on various religious denominations and the subscriptions of those in Wales who had faith in the educational future of the country. In 1880 a Commission of Inquiry into higher education in Wales was established under the chairmanship of Lord Aberdare, a barrister who had been Home Secretary in Gladstone's first government in 1868, and who was raised to the peerage on becoming Lord President of the Council in 1873. The Aberdare Commission recommended that two university colleges should be established; one in North Wales and one in South Wales, and that both should receive the substantial grant of £4,000 per annum from the Treasury. As a direct consequence, by 1883 the movement for the foundation of the North Wales college had become clearly defined under the dynamic leadership of William Rathbone, the Liberal Member of Parliament for Carnarvonshire. Rathbone, previously M.P. for Liverpool from 1868 to 1880, was not only a founder of the Liverpool Royal Infirmary, but in 1882 he was a principal founding benefactor of University College, Liverpool. He was ideally qualified to lead the college foundation movement in his new constituency. He had the foresight to engage, at his own expense, the 31 year old Henry Jones, lecturer in Philosophy at the Aberystwyth college, to assist in the drafting of a constitution for the proposed new college.

Jones, later Sir Henry Jones, a native of Llangernyw in Denbighshire, had been a student at Bangor Normal College, a teacher for two years in South Wales, and then a student of philosophy at the University of Glasgow. A fellowship at Glasgow had led to a lectureship at Aberystwyth. The combination of Rathbone and Jones, the former an uncompromising English Liberal free trader of Quaker heritage, and the latter a Welsh Calvinistic Methodist, destined to become perhaps the greatest moral philosopher of his day, provided the new University College at Bangor from its very inception with a valuable diversity of outlook and experience. To their liberal nonconformity was almost immediately added a counter-weight of conservative Anglicanism and educational tradition represented by Colonel the Hon. William Sackville-West M.A., who was nominated by the University of Oxford as their representative on the Bangor Court of Governors. Given this varied input to its foundation, it was perhaps not surprising that when the Royal Charter of the University College was granted, the stated mission of the college was 'to provide instruction in all the branches of a liberal education except theology'.

The decision to site the University College in Bangor was certainly not merely a reflection of the city's history as an ancient monastic and cultural centre on the Menai Strait dating back to the Dark Ages. It had already been the home of the greatly admired Normal College for nearly 40 years, but more importantly, it enjoyed good communications, being on the main railway line to London. Bangor had remained the centre of railway engineering for the Chester and Holyhead Railway, later part of the London & North Western Railway, since its completion by Robert Stephenson in 1850. By 1884 branch lines linked Bangor to Caernarfon (1857) and thence via the Nantlle railway to the slate quarries of that area. The great slate-quarrying communities of Llanberis and Bethesda were linked to Bangor in 1869 and 1884 respectively. Branch lines in Anglesey had linked Llanerchymedd and Amlwch to Bangor in 1867. This great improvement in lines of communication into Bangor was a consequence mainly of the slate-quarrying industry, then at its peak, which employed, directly and indirectly over 25,000 workers. Not surprisingly, therefore, in view of the educational potential it was to provide for their sons, the quarrymen of Carnarvonshire contributed handsomely to the University College of Bangor. The workers of Penrhyn Quarry at Bethesda alone subscribed over £1,000 to the college.

Other subscriptions included a thousand pounds from each of seven wealthy benefactors at a meeting held at Chester in early 1883 to open a public subscription list. The contributors were the Duke of Westminster, Lord Penrhyn, Mr William Rathbone M.P., Mr Richard Davies of Treborth M.P., Mr John Roberts, solicitor of Bangor, Sir Henry Tate of Liverpool, and Mr R.S. Hudson of Chester. A link between the College and the established Church in Bangor was remarkably forged by the Dean of Bangor, the Very Reverend H.T. Edwards, who has been described as "one of the staunchest friends of the College at the time of its foundation, and one of the most eloquent advocates of its claims upon the support of the country". Writing retrospectively in 1905, the first Registrar of the College, W. Cadwaladr Davies and Professor Lewis Jones, in their book *The University of Wales*, go on to refer to Dean Edwards' campaign in Anglesey on behalf of the college establishment fund as "one of the most dramatic incidents of the whole movement".

It was, however, stated by Davies and Jones, "that of all the benefactors of the Bangor College … William Rathbone, its second President, stands in honourable and unchallenged pre-eminence. The amount of Mr Rathbone's money contributions to various College funds … exceeded that of any other of its friends … but his services, whether to the College or Welsh education generally, are not to be assessed as equivalent to so many pounds sterling" Fifty years later, the anniversary celebration booklet published in 1934, referred to Rathbone's "unflagging faith and energy" which had so greatly contributed to the progress of the college. It also recalled the view of the college's first Principal that Sir William Rathbone had earned the title of 'Father of the College'.

The first meeting of the Council of the University College of North Wales took place on March 8th 1884. Those present included the Earl of Powis, a devoted classical scholar, High Steward of the University of Cambridge, and an active and influential figure at Westminster (President of the College and of the Court of Governors), Richard Davies M.P. of Treborth Hall (Vice-President of the

College and of the Court of Governors), Col. The Hon. William Sackville-West (Chairman of Council) and William Rathbone M.P. (Vice-Chairman of Council). These four were the principal founders of the College and included its main benefactor. Also in attendance as Council members were J.R. Davies M.A., J.P., son of Richard Davies M.P.; Arthur Wyatt, J.P.; Thomas Gee, publisher, of Denbigh; the Rev. Daniel Rowlands of Bangor Normal College, and Captain Edmund Verney R.N., M.P. for Anglesey from 1886. Of the above, five are known to have been friends of the Vincents and appear in the Diary.

With wisdom and optimism, the college founders thought it imprudent to spend large amounts of the money subscribed on new buildings, given the confident hope that the institution would develop rapidly, and perhaps in unpredictable directions. They sought therefore to appoint a staff notable for its teaching excellence and to defer new buildings until the College had achieved some degree of recognised success. Accommodation was obtained through a long generous lease from Lord Penrhyn of what had been the well-known coaching inn, the Penrhyn Arms Hotel, at the lower end of Bangor. The additional buildings required to house laboratories for the natural and physical sciences were constructed in its curtilage.

The academic staff of the new University College of North Wales. Principal Harry Reichel is seated centre, Professor Henry Jones is seated second left. The Diary records visits from Mr E.J. Trechmann (seated first left) and Mr E.V. Arnold (first right, middle row). (University of Wales, Bangor)

43

At a meeting of the College Council in May 1884, held at the Queen's Head Café in Bangor High Street, the most critical appointment was made. Mr H.R. Reichel, a young fellow of All Souls, Oxford, was appointed both Principal and Professor of English and History. At the following meeting in early June of that year, held at the Queen Hotel in Chester, the Council appointed five professors. These were Mr J.J. Dobbie, M.A. Glasgow, D.Sc Edinburgh (Chemistry and Geology); Mr G. Ballard Matthews, B.A., Cambridge (Mathematics); Mr Andrew Gray, M.A., Glasgow, FRSE (Physics); Mr W. Rhys Roberts, M.A., Cambridge (Classics); and the previously mentioned Mr Henry Jones, M.A., Glasgow (Logic, Philosophy and Political Economy). Within a year or two, three lecturers were appointed: Mr R.W. Phillips, B.A., B.Sc., (who went on to become Professor of Biology in 1888); Mr E.J. Trechmann, B.A., Ph.D., lecturer in Modern Languages (who later went as a professor to the University of Sydney), and Mr E.V. Arnold, M.A., Fellow of Trinity College Cambridge (who became Professor of Latin in 1888). With the appointment of the latter, Professor William Rhys Roberts became solely Professor of Greek. This auspicious intellectual group greatly added to the cultural and social life of the city of Bangor. They quickly made friends outside the immediate college community and several of them are mentioned in a social context in the Vincent Diary.

The College opened officially on October 14th 1884 with 58 students registered. It was a provision of the College Charter that female students should be admitted to the courses of instruction and indeed, the very first student enrolled was a Mary Ellen Williams of Bangor. This first intake of students included the two younger Vincent girls, Eva and Georgie; their friends, Lionel, Mary and Cecilie Sackville-West; Margaret Louisa Wyatt; Mary Rathbone, the niece of William Rathbone; and two daughters of Richard Davies of Treborth Hall, Katie and Edith. The College provided unprecedented opportunities for the furthering of existing friendships within the Bangor community and for the fostering of new acquaintance irrespective of background. For local middle-class girls it represented a revelation of opportunity. Whereas traditionally their brothers went away for higher education, it was now coming to them. Women students also came to Bangor from far afield, and were able to compete for scholarships generously provided by the Worshipful Company of Drapers in London. Men students also entered the college from a broad range of the social spectrum.

A survey of the first hundred students enrolled within the first full academic year reveals several interesting facts. The group comprised 61 men and

39 women. Eighty students came from North Wales, 10 from elsewhere in Wales and 10 from England and Scotland. As many as 60 of the North Wales students were from Bangor and its immediate area and 15% of these were the sons of slate quarrymen. At least 52 of the first 100 students are known to have proceeded to degrees, mostly by examination as external candidates of the University of London. Eight of these degrees went to women students. Of the men, 19 became clergymen. Nine of the students, 8 men and 1 woman, essentially used Bangor to follow a pre-medical course, before proceeding to graduate, mostly from Edinburgh.

One such Edinburgh medical graduate – a quarryman's son from Ffestiniog – was student Number 37, Robert Morris Williams, who upon graduation, returned to North Wales and established his practice at Hawthorn House in Menai Bridge town. It is difficult to imagine how, without the presence of a college in Bangor, it would have been possible for a quarryman's son to have attained such professional status at this time.

Twenty of this first student entry eventually went into education, including three professors, two directors of education and several head teachers. This is indeed a proud record for any such newly established institution. Many of the young women probably had no intention of following a degree course, but were, nevertheless, serious students. For example, Mary and Cecilie Sackville-West attended the college for 19 and 13 terms respectively. Their education would have been a significant asset when the one married a Member of Parliament and the other, the vice-principal of Keble College, Oxford. Their brother Lionel, on the other hand, spent only three terms at Bangor where he matriculated before proceeding to Oxford.

The market for the North Wales college was, therefore, almost immediately apparent, and the extent of demand from the Bangor area itself was particularly gratifying to the supporters and authorities of the college. The institution grew and attracted students from further and further afield. As a consequence, the life and economy of the small city were radically altered for ever. The founding of the University College of North Wales at Bangor was, without doubt, the most important single factor in the modern history of the city. Bangor was one of the very few Victorian University institutions in Britain that were not established in large centres of concentrated population. As a consequence, town and gown enjoyed the advantage of an intimate, self-contained social life, in which the young Vincents were witnesses and participants.

7. THE NATION IN 1885 and 1886

Political and Economic Concerns

The dawn of the year 1885 saw Queen Victoria in the forty-eighth year of her reign, and Mr Gladstone, in his seventy-sixth year, nearing the end of his second term as prime minister. His Liberal government was under heavy pressure over a number of issues. Overseas the British Empire was moving towards its territorial peak, but at home there were problems. Agriculture was in the midst of a twenty-year depression. British farmers were suffering from the low price of wheat and were complaining about the monopolistic profits charged by the middlemen who passed on their produce to the general public. The result of this slump was that the acreage under wheat in 1885 was the smallest then on record, and the farmers' problems were exacerbated by heavy September rains which ruined a great proportion of the crop. Falling profits from trade and industry also contributed to what many historians have termed "The Great Depression".

The year 1884 had seen an almost complete cessation of shipbuilding in Britain and 1885 added to a long list of bad years for the iron and steel industries. The price of ship-quality steel plate declined from £7 per ton in early 1885 to 10 shillings per ton at the end of the year. Likewise, the copper industry suffered heavy losses with very large quantities of unsold stock, and the British chemical industry was described by *The Times* as having suffered "an exhausting monotony of dullness and decline". In Manchester the trade unions fought against a five per cent reduction in the wages of their workers in the Lancashire cotton industry. The sugar business was one of the few to remain relatively prosperous. The Revenue returns for 1884 and 1885 were thought by many to be misleading. In particular, the Treasury was criticised for devising technical changes which made year to year comparisons difficult if not impossible. No social class went completely untouched by the depression, and it was in this decade that the modern concept of unemployment came into being and during which emigration to both North America and Australasia accelerated.

Despite the Depression, Britain still far outstripped the other industrial nations in coal production. The decade up to 1884 had seen a productivity increase of 40%, which served to meet export demands and supply the coaling stations of the Empire. The winning of coal was not without its human cost. In South Wales at the end of 1885, a massive explosion at the Maerdy Colliery near

Ferndale caused the death of over 80 miners. Six months earlier 179 lives had been lost in the Clifton Hall Colliery explosion at Pendlebury near Manchester. Coroners' verdicts of accidental death were condemned in *The Times* for January 5th 1886 as "a sham, a mockery, a delusion and a positive evil" in view of the fact that government inspectors' warnings against the use of naked lights had gone unheeded in both places.

Nevertheless, the heaviest cloud on the economic horizon was increasing competition, mainly from German industry and American agriculture. Britain was no longer "the workshop of the world". Imperial expansion was at least one means of assuring additional protected markets for Britain and of bolstering the nation's faltering self-confidence.

Public concerns were strongly expressed and opinions were polarized over the issue of Irish Home Rule. The Fenians, an Irish-American organization, had brought terrorist outrage to the British mainland over the previous two decades. The year 1885 was to see a renewed campaign of bomb attacks in London. On January 2nd there was such an outrage on the underground near Gower Street. This was followed by three almost simultaneous dynamite explosions on January 24th at the Tower of London, Westminster Hall and the House of Commons. It was reported by the press that these were timed to occur at 2 o'clock in the afternoon, a time when visitors would be likely to be gathered in great numbers. These particularly destructive explosions had followed similar attacks on government buildings and the offices of *The Times* in March 1883, and on the underground at Paddington and Westminster in October 1883. During 1884 there had been a spate of bombings at St James' Square, Scotland Yard, London Bridge, and at Victoria, Paddington and King's Cross stations.

In foreign affairs, the government was criticised for having neglected the country's interests in such places as Egypt, the Sudan, southern Africa and the Pacific rim. Gladstone had reluctantly annexed Egypt in 1882 in order to protect the Suez Canal, partially owned by the British Government and essential for the British link to India. Having assumed control of Egypt, the British Government had failed to suppress revolt in the Sudan, which had placed both Egyptian soldiers and civilians in grave danger. With the realisation in 1883 that the Egyptians could not be left to the mercy of the Sudanese rebels, General Gordon had been sent to Khartoum to report on and organize the best method of their evacuation. He was accompanied by just one British officer. Gordon arrived in February 1884 and successfully organized the evacuation of two and a half thousand Egyptian women and children before being besieged by the forces of the Mahdi. The British Government vacillated, and Gordon and the Egyptian troops were essentially abandoned until reinforcements were belatedly despatched. His brilliant defence of Khartoum lasted for almost a year until early 1885. *The Times* for January 2nd 1885 reported a message, "Khartoum all right. December 14th. C.G. Gordon", and went on to quote the messenger as saying that General Gordon had personally told him that "Khartoum could not be taken by the enemy."

In Africa south of the equator, British concern for the safety of the Cape Colony was aroused by German claims that the possessions of the Boers and Germans in South Africa might soon be formed into a chain of non-British territory extending from the Atlantic to the Indian Ocean. This fear was justified by Prince Bismarck's claim to have absorbed territory from the Atlantic coast up the Orange River in South West Africa, and also to have obtained a foothold on the Indian Ocean coast of Kwazulu. The situation was, however, confused when news broke on January 1st 1885 that the Transvaal government of Paul Kruger had stated that they would strenuously oppose every attempt at the annexation of Zululand territory by either Germany or England.

There were further worries about German colonial ambitions in the south-west Pacific Ocean, notably in the eastern part of New Guinea and the New Hebrides. In London, the Australian Agent-General for Victoria vigorously protested against the recognition of German claims in New Guinea and declared that if the territory was not claimed back by Britain, and if the British presence in the New Hebrides was not similarly guaranteed, there would be a feeling of deep estrangement from the mother country on the part of colonists in the region.

Further threats to the British Empire emanated from St Petersburg, where, according to *The Times* on January 3rd 1885, "expert opinion in Central Asian affairs" called for the necessity of acquisition of India by Russia. The Russian objective was to pressurize Britain in order to guarantee year-round access to the world's oceans via the Bosporous. The report quoted a Russian military source:

> The possibility of an invasion of India is a source of great agitation in England, and well may it be so, for whoever deals England a blow there sounds her death-knell. England's immense trade in the east is entirely dependent on her possession of Hindostan. There is scarcely a well to-do English family or commercial firm that is not more or less dependent upon Indian trade or occupation in the Indian service... The same causes that destroyed ancient

Carthage will also bring down the British Empire. More than 250 millions of souls are simply English slaves. All England's possessions are simply held for what she can get out of them. Every vestige of justice and magnanimity has disappeared from the British administration in India. Justice in India is a farce. As to how an invasion of India is to be accomplished, we leave the English to find out our plans…

The style of this rhetoric may have been laughable but the threat was perceived as genuine, and added to the general feeling of unease in the country and lack of public confidence in the government. As a result of this apprehension about the future, it was not uncommon for the constitution of the United Kingdom to be questioned. There was a perceived need for the extension of political privilege. It was also widely felt that both politicians and civil servants should be required to demonstrate a greater sense of public responsibility. *The Times*, on January 1st 1885, declared that the advent of a greater degree of democracy such as that achieved by Gladstone's 1884 Reform Act, which gave the vote to agricultural labourers, would lead to a more just, generous, and more enlightened policy towards the overseas empire. Its effects at home were more immediate. The price exacted by the Tory opposition for the Bill's successful passage through the House of Lords, where they had a majority, was the redrawing of urban and suburban constituency boundaries. As they hoped, this eventually worked to the Tory advantage in the general election of late 1885.

In the meantime, however, Gladstone created political turmoil in June 1885 by resigning, ostensibly due to a defeat on a budget amendment. The real issue, as so often, was Ireland. Salisbury reluctantly formed a minority Conservative administration, and then went to the country in November 1885. Gladstone's Liberals were again the largest single party with a majority of 86 over the Conservatives, but the Irish Home Rule Party, led by Charles Parnell, benefiting from the extension of the franchise to agricultural workers in Ireland, found themselves with precisely 86 MPs and holding the balance of power in the House of Commons. Salisbury continued until defeated in parliament in January 1886, and Gladstone returned to power without an election but with a clear commitment to a Dublin parliament with complete responsibility for internal affairs. This issue was to split the Liberal Party and change the face of British politics. When this Irish Home Rule Bill went to the House in the summer of 1886, 93 Liberals voted with the Conservatives against the Bill and brought Gladstone down by 30 votes. It was at this time that the Vincents' friend, Richard Davies, felt that he could no longer support Gladstone and resigned his Anglesey seat.

The ensuing general election of July 1886 saw the return of Salisbury with 316 Conservative members compared with Gladstone's 191 Liberal seats. In addition, Salisbury could count on the support of the 78 Unionist Liberals led by Joseph Chamberlain, who aligned themselves with the Conservatives under the Anti-Home Rule Coalition banner. Parnell's Irish Home Rule Party still had 85 seats but had lost their influence. The Conservatives dominated British politics for much of the next twenty years.

The Contemporary Arts

In addition to the amateur musical talents of the Vincent daughters, the whole family appear to have been well-read. Several of them also greatly enjoyed the theatre. Ted, through his recent marriage, was already moving in literary and theatrical circles that included the younger Irvings. There are family records of both Hugh and William Vincent attending performances at the new Theatre Royal, the Queen's Theatre and the Gaiety while students in Dublin, and Mollie seems to have gone to the theatre whenever visiting Dublin or London.

By the 1880s the theatre had become respectable and immensely popular with the middle-class. The bawdy had been banished to the music halls, and melodrama marginalised to theatres in working-class areas. The West End and major provincial theatres offered a menu of the classics, drawing-room comedy and farce, which became the rage after the enormous success in 1885 of *The Magistrate* by Arthur Wing Pinero at the Court Theatre.

At this period, autocratic actor managers reigned supreme. The year 1885 saw the retirement of the great husband and wife partnership of Squire and Marie Bancroft, who had enjoyed a highly successful career at the Haymarket. The Bancrofts were responsible for many artistic and managerial innovations that had done much to transform the British theatre and the public image of actors. Charles Wyndham was successfully managing the Criterion, and John Hare and William Kendall were in partnership at the St James' Theatre.

The most illustrious of them all, however, was Henry Irving whose leading lady was Ellen Terry. In 1884 they toured Canada and the United States and returned for their sixth season at London's Lyceum Theatre with *Much Ado About Nothing* and *Twelfth Night*. Mollie Vincent saw this production of *Much Ado* and recorded her memories of the performance:

Ellen Terry looked on the stage most lovely and most sweet, nothing could be more graceful than her figure and the first tone of her voice makes one feel happy. Her dresses were most beautiful: one a rich white brocade and the other a golden brown brocade. I don't know what the real colour of her hair may be but that night it was light, done high up on her head and curled in front. She had her bodices cut square, with a large high ruff. Irving is an ugly long thin man, with dark eyes and a hooked nose. He did not look young at all in spite of being dressed as if he was. When you hear his voice at first you hate it and his accent is most peculiar but after a time you get accustomed to it, and one cannot but feel that good or bad, his acting helps one to understand Shakespeare more than one thought one ever could.

In 1885 the repertoire at the Lyceum was *Hamlet* and a revival of *Olivia*, an adaptation of *The Vicar of Wakefield* which had been an earlier triumph for Ellen Terry with another company. This new and very successful production boasted incidental music by Arthur Sullivan, and was the theatrical highlight of Mollie and Will Vincent's visit to London in July of that year.

The famous collaboration between William Gilbert and Arthur Sullivan had begun back in the 1870s. Such was the success of their light operas that the impresario, Richard D'Oyly Carte opened the Savoy Theatre for the performance of what became known as the Savoy Operas. The first production at the Savoy was *Patience* in 1881, and in 1885 Mollie and Will went there to see *The Mikado*. The phenomenal popularity of Gilbert and Sullivan spread to Europe and the United States, adding to the prestige of the English theatre.

The new respectability of the professional theatre made it acceptable for the middle and upper classes to participate in amateur dramatics. 'Theatricals' were often included in the invitations received by the Vincents. In April 1885 they attended such an event at Gorddinog, the boyhood home of their father, which was now owned by Colonel Henry Platt. Although the performance of *Old Soldiers* was purely amateur, the Platts had the programme for the production specially printed in London. The Vincents were entertained by one of their more colourful friends, Norris Wyatt, in one of the leading roles. The performance was repeated two days later in Caernarfon for the benefit of the local lifeboat, an example of how the Victorians combined recreation and charity.

There is no evidence that any of the Vincents drew or painted like their friends the Davies and Ramsay girls, but earlier diary fragments at least show that Mollie attended exhibitions in Dublin and London. It is perhaps surprising that she did not include a gallery visit when she went to London in 1885, because during the last quarter of the nineteenth century, art in Britain was enjoying a level of popularity that was unprecedented and never to be repeated. The Royal Academy drew huge crowds, and its Summer Exhibition was very much part of the London Season. British painting was dominated by the Academy's president, Sir Frederick Leighton. His painting *Captive Andromache* was exhibited at the Academy in 1885, the year in which he received his baronetcy. His fellow neo-classicist, Lawrence Alma-Tadema was also enjoying great popularity and success. His painting *An Apodyterium* was voted Picture of the Year for 1886, and *Expectations,* painted in 1885, went on to win the gold medal at the Paris Exposition Universelle of 1889.

Edward Burne-Jones finally achieved an international reputation in the 1880s. His highly successful *King Cophetua and the Beggar Maid* was painted in 1884 and during the middle years of the decade he was in great demand for his stained-glass window designs. These were for churches both grand and humble, and included *The Ascension* and *The Resurrection* for St Philip's Cathedral, Birmingham. At this time he also designed the mosaics for the ceiling of the apse of the American Episcopal Church of St Paul in Rome. Much closer to the Vincent home, one of Burne-Jones' window designs is to be found in the Church of St Cross on the Penrhyn estate just outside the village of Talybont, near Bangor. A beautiful east window was commissioned for the church, which was built by Lord Penrhyn for his estate workers and tenants. A central lancet depicts the Crucifixion and is flanked by images of St Mary and St John.

The idea that art should not be accessible and popular, that the artist belonged to an aesthetic and intellectual elite, standing outside society, as a critical and potentially subversive figure, was beginning to appear with the Aesthetic movement. Its chief exponent in Britain, however, the waspish and dandified J.M. Whistler, was still regarded at this time as an eccentric and often found himself the butt of popular satire. The painters that the public loved, men such as Leighton, Alma-Tadema, Millais, Burne-Jones and Waterhouse, spanned many different schools of art and did not always win critical acclaim, but they gave the late Victorians the pictures they wanted. These were idealised images of the past, be it classical, medieval or pre-industrial Arcadian. In return, they were feted by society, earned great wealth and were showered with honours, created knights, baronets and, in the case of Leighton, a peer of the realm.

Musical ability, in singing or playing an instrument, was rated very highly as a social accomplishment, particularly for young women. It is known that Mollie took singing lessons well into her twenties and that Lil played the piano. The piano was the most popular instrument and every home that could possibly afford it, had one. The sales of sheet music at this time were booming. It is hard to credit from a modern standpoint, but when the Vincent girls met their friends to play classical music, they were often indulging in the Victorian equivalent of getting together to listen to the latest popular releases. Brahms, who appears frequently in the programmes of the Bangor Amateur Music Society, was very much the pop star of his day.

Such had been the public adulation received by Brahms when he visited Britain in 1884 that *The Times,* reviewing European music at the beginning of 1885, rather peevishly took exception to the "excessive admiration of Brahms worshippers, which places his symphonies on a level of the masterpieces of Beethoven, or even of Schumann and Schubert". The newspaper referred to the manner in which the "towering genius of Wagner [*who had died in 1883*] continues to cast its shadow on the efforts of his countrymen as did that of Beethoven fifty years ago". It did, however, rather grudgingly admit that the first performance of Brahms' Third Symphony in F "must be classed among the memorable events of the musical year". March 1884 had seen the first performance of Dvorak's Symphony in D, conducted at the Philarmonic Society by the composer, and his *Stabat Mater* had been performed at the Albert Hall during this, his first visit to Britain. Despite all of this, and the appearance of Bruckner's 7th Symphony, which does not even get a mention, *The Times* stated dismissively that 1884 "is not likely to be favourably remembered in the annals of music and there is reason to doubt whether it has produced a single work which future ages will not be willing to let die".

British writers in the mid -1880s produced many works which have since become classics. Robert Louis Stevenson's *Treasure Island* had appeared in 1883; he followed this in 1885 with *A Child's Garden of Verses* and in 1886 he published both *Kidnapped* and *Dr Jekyll and Mr Hyde.* The unexpurgated version of Richard Burton's translation of *The Arabian Nights* was published in 1885, as was the highly popular adventure *King Solomon's Mines* by Rider Haggard. In 1886 Thomas Hardy brought out his tenth novel, T*he Mayor of Casterbridge* and the 21-year-old journalist, Rudyard Kipling, embarked on his literary career with the publication of *Departmental Ditties.* Two great Victorian poets were nearing the end of their long and illustrious careers. In 1884 the 72-year-old Robert Browning published *Ferishtah's Fancies* and Alfred, Lord Tennyson, who had succeeded Wordsworth as Poet Laureate back in 1850, produced *Tiresias* in 1885 at the age of 76. He followed it in 1886 with *Locksley Hall Sixty Years On,* a sequel to his *Locksley Hall* which had appeared 44 years earlier in 1842.

Advances in Science

In its review of science in 1885, *The Times* for January 8th 1886 referred to the erection of a statue of Charles Darwin in the Natural History Museum as "a notable event from many points of view" and as "one more proof of the dominating influence which science has attained". Society was increasingly looking to science to solve its problems and explain the world. For the most part science was delivering. The years 1884 and 1885 were particularly notable for important new developments in micro-biological and medical research. In Germany in 1884, Robert Koch who had already discovered the anthrax bacillus and that of tuberculosis, announced and described his discovery of cholera and produced the first pure culture of the bacterium. Louis Pasteur, the French chemist, introduced the technique of inoculation as a preventative treatment for the rabies virus in dogs and resultant hydrophobia in man. The result of Pasteur's work was a reduction of the death rate from the disease to less than one per cent of its former level.

In the 1880s Britain was blessed with a wealth of eminent scientists, especially in the field of physics. Lord Rayleigh, who had brought precise mathematical analysis to so many branches of both experimental and theoretical physics, retired as Professor of Physics at the University of Cambridge in 1884. He was succeeded by J.J. Thomson, who was to become the discoverer of the electron. It was the presence of Thomson as Cavendish Professor of Experimental Physics at Cambridge that was later to attract Ernest Rutherford, the 'Father of Nuclear Physics', to the university. The year also saw a new treatise on light by Professor Sir William Stokes. Perhaps the highlight of the year in physics, however, was the series of lectures delivered at Johns Hopkins University in Baltimore on the Wave Theory of Light, by Sir William Thomson, later Lord Kelvin, who was Professor of Natural Philosophy at the University of Glasgow for 53 years and recognised as one of the greatest physicists of his time. It was he whom the new University College of Bangor invited to open its science laboratories in 1885.

The greatest British biologist of the day, Professor Thomas Huxley, was President of the Royal Society from 1881 to 1885. One of his most influential books, *Science and Morals*, in which he attempted to define the conflicting relationship between the philosophy of science and that of religion appeared in 1885. Sir Richard Owen the eminent palaeontologist completed his great work on *Fossil Vertebrates* in 1884. The same year also saw the publication of several volumes on the results of the world voyage of *HMS Challenger*, which provided revolutionary knowledge of the deep marine sedimentary deposits on the ocean floors and of the nature of life in the oceans.

The mid-1880s was a period when Nature herself was unusually active. The year 1884 was one of remarkable sunsets caused by the catastrophic explosion of the volcano Krakatoa in the previous year. On no other occasion had a natural explosion ever been heard at places 3,000 miles from its source, and the tidal wave generated was readily detected nearly 8,000 miles away at Cape Horn. *The Times,* while noting that "volcanoes inevitably suggest earthquakes, which were it not for the disasters they bring to humanity, would be welcome as important phenomena for scientific investigation," commented upon the spate of earthquakes which had been suffered by Spain in 1884. *The Times* also highlighted the study of the earth when it referred to the meticulous mapping work of the officers of the Geological Survey in Scotland, where discoveries in the Northwest Highlands had shed totally fresh light upon the understanding of the nature and structure of the world's mountain ranges.

Perhaps the technological development with the greatest long-term consequence for modern society was taking place in Germany. This led to the patenting by Karl Benz in January 1886 of the first petrol-driven motor car.

Religious Doubt and Debate

Of all the national institutions, the one to which the Vincent family was most devoted for over five generations, was the Anglican Church in Wales. Very much in keeping with the questioning spirit of the age, the Established Church by the 1880s was coming under attack from several directions and this would have been a frequent topic of conversation among the family and their friends. The Anglican Church had been disestablished in Ireland in 1869, during the first year of the first Gladstone government, and it was perhaps inevitable that the Church was having to defend its established position in England and Wales.

There was no denying that the Church in all its manifestations, Established or otherwise, had been deeply wounded by the perceived conflict between religion and the natural sciences precipitated by the publication of *The Origin of Species* in 1859. This had been inflamed at the British Association meeting of 1860 at Oxford, by the confrontation between Samuel Wilberforce, Bishop of Oxford, and Professor Thomas Huxley, the champion of Darwinism.

The scientific questioning of the Old Testament account of creation added to earlier attacks by German biblical scholars on the historical accuracy of the New Testament. The danger was that once the authority of the Bible was challenged, the Church could become an irrelevance. "Doubt" became a major issue among the educated classes. The Anglican Church was also losing the working classes. The industrial revolution continued to cause the movement of many working people from the strong parish structure of the countryside to the industrial centres where their faith frequently either lapsed or was revived by Nonconformism. The Anglican Church had been shocked out of its complacency by the results of the 1851 census which had asked, for the first and last time, about people's church attendance. This had revealed that only 35% of the population attended any kind of worship, and only just over half of these were Anglican.

The essential problem, across the classes and for whatever reason, was unbelief, which had spread quickly in the 1870s. Figures gathered in the 1880s showed that although 75% of children in England and Wales attended Sunday schools, church attendance by their parents was in significant decline. At the beginning of the decade, recognising the problem, William Magee, the Bishop of Peterborough (and a half-brother of Grace Vincent's father, the Rev. William Johnson), when chairing the Church Congress, stated "the religious condition of the masses" was "the one great Church question of our time, before which, all others fade into insignificance".

From the early 1880s, Anglican thinkers began to fight back. Widely read New Testament commentaries by Joseph Lightfoot and Brooke Westcott, two Cambridge academics who both went on to become Bishops of Durham, did much to repair the damage done by the German scholars. Others of their contemporaries argued that the conflict between religion and science was much overstated, and that Darwin was no enemy of the Church. It is worthy of note that in *The Origin of Species* Darwin had stated that he saw "no good reason why the views given in this volume should shock the religious feelings of anyone." By the late 1880s, Anglicans had come to share the opinion of Cardinal John Henry Newman, who back in 1868 had stated that "Mr Darwin's theory need not then be atheistical." Thus the Anglican Church came to adjust its thinking to accommodate the evolutionary concept and other new scientific knowledge.

The loss of the educated classes from the Anglican Church was at least staunched, but it was in danger of becoming an essentially middle and upper class institution. With fewer than 20% of the population attending its services regularly, its position as the Established Church was increasingly questioned. The political battle over disestablishment continued to rumble on and was the cause of much pain and acrimony, especially in Wales.

*

How then did these large issues impinge upon the lives of the Vincents living in a quiet corner of North Wales? The family's income came from the farming of their modest estate, but the depression in agriculture at this time was less serious in North Wales than elsewhere. Mixed farming and cattle and sheep grazing were less vulnerable than, for example, the cereal production of eastern England. The largest source of employment in North Wales was the slate industry which was still at a peak of production with a large domestic, European and imperial market. In all its aspects of roofing slate production, ancillary products, associated foundries, distribution and shipping, the industry employed well over 25,000 men in a relatively compact area with reasonably good communications.

The shipping line founded by the Vincents' friends, the Davieses of Treborth Hall, was at its most successful in the 1880s. There were 20 ships in service with a total unladen weight of over 25,000 tons. By this period, the shipping of coal from Cardiff and Swansea to California and returning with grain or the natural fertilizer, Peruvian guano, was reaching its peak. It was in 1887-8 that the Davies ship *Merioneth*, under its famous master, Captain Robert Thomas of Llandwrog, Caernarfon, broke all records for the passage from Europe to San Francisco, completing the voyage in 96 days. Viewed from North Wales, the nation's economic problems probably seemed somewhat remote.

The fears of the English Bishops must have seemed equally distant. Bangor was a very small city and its Cathedral exerted a considerable influence both locally and throughout its large rural diocese. The Penrhyn family and other large estate owners were still providing and maintaining new churches for their tenants and workers right up to the end of the century, and the plethora of chapels built in and around Bangor at this period bears witness to the strength of the Nonconformist communities. The deeply-felt rivalry between Church and Chapel in Wales may well have served to keep their respective congregations faithful. The Vincents were conscientious about their Sunday observance, only poor health keeping members of the family away. If bad weather made the three-mile drive or walk to the Cathedral unattractive, they would attend service at one of the more local parish churches.

In many ways the provinces a hundred years ago were not at all parochial in their outlook and attitudes. The editorial pages of the *North Wales Chronicle* of

57

the day were dedicated almost entirely to the relaying of national and international news, and there was a strong sense of identification with other parts of the country. The United Kingdom was very much united. Thanks to the railways, people and news travelled quickly. The Diaries and other family records show that the Vincents travelled widely and had friends throughout the country. They even shared the fear of Irish terrorism. The two bridges across the Menai Strait which were such a vital link in the communication between London and Dublin, were seen as particularly vulnerable and were often guarded. In no way would the Vincents have felt geographically or socially isolated.

Part Four : Daily Life

---

8. THE VINCENT FAMILY DIARY

On Christmas Day 1884, Grace Vincent received from her young neighbour, Edith Davies, the gift of a thick, hard-back writing book. Perhaps the Vincents were in the habit of keeping a diary, and earlier volumes have been lost over the years; perhaps it was a Davies family tradition that the Vincents had expressed a wish to emulate and the gift was meant as encouragement.

What we can be sure of is that as the year turned, Grace Vincent, who was now 56 years old, had all her family about her. Her eldest child, Ted, was now 27 and had come home for the holiday period with Babs, his bride of five months. As a barrister and journalist, however, he was now permanently resident in London. Lil Vincent was 24 and her fiancé, Jack Lloyd-Williams, was staying with the family at Treborth. They were to marry seven months later. Hugh, now 22, had returned to live at home after completing his arts degree at Trinity College Dublin the previous summer. Serving his articles was often taking him to London and as his career became established he would inevitably leave home. Will, at the age of 18, was mostly in London preparing for the Indian Civil Service entrance examinations. Success would take him to university and ultimately to India for many years at a time without home leave. Even Gustie, the baby of the family, was now 16 and about to enrol for courses in Greek, Mathematics and French at the new University College in Bangor, with ambitions to join the army, which would certainly take him away from home. Grace must also have hoped that her three other daughters Mollie who was by now 25, Eva aged 20 and Georgie just 17, would all marry.

So perhaps it was a sense that such occasions with all her children together would become increasingly rare that made her feel she wished her family's activities to be recorded. Consequently, she passed the writing book to her eldest daughter, Mollie, and charged her with the responsibility of keeping The Vincent Family Diary.

THE VINCENT FAMILY DIARY FOR 1885

"At home on New Year's Day 1885:

The Mother, Edmund, Mary, (alias Babs), Mollie, Lil, Jack, Hugh, Eva, Will, Georgie and Gustie.

"Eva, Mollie, Will and Gustie came from a dance at Llanfaethlu [*western Anglesey*]. Lil and Jack drove to Bangor. Babs came to help Mollie and look over her dress. Edmund in Bangor at Mr Barber's [*solicitor's*] office. Eva not well, had to go to bed. Dr Prydderch [*Hugh Prydderch MRCS, LRCP, of Bridge Street, Menai Bridge*] was sent for. Mr Owen Evans and Mary came to call and had tea [*Mr Owen Evans was Minor Canon at Bangor Cathedral, Mary was his sister*]. Mr Hamilton Poole called. Frank Watkin-Davies came for the dance at Lime Grove. We dined and afterwards dressed. Babs had on her wedding dress, Georgie her bridesmaid's dress (white and yellow). Our party consisted of Edmund, Mollie, Georgie, Hugh, Will, Gus and Frank Davies. We got home at about 3 o'clock and the game was quite worth the candle."

Friday, January 2nd:

"Frank Watkin-Davies went away and Hugh came back from Penrallt [*the Bangor home of the Barber family, where he had spent the night*]. Edmund, Hugh and Gus played a football match at Beaumaris. All very tired, but went to the Davieses' [*Treborth Hall*] in the evening and read *Much Ado About Nothing*."

Sunday, January 4th:

"Mother, Jack, Lil and Georgie went to the Cathedral. Eva did not go out. Everyone had colds. Lil to Penrhos [*church*] in the evening."

Monday, January 5th:

"Babs and Will back to London. [*Edmund remained in Bangor on business.*] Mr Hamilton Poole came to dinner. Dancing for an hour. Bed."

Tuesday, January 6th:

"Annie Barber and Cecilie Sackville-West came over and talked with Mollie in her room, everyone else had bad colds."

Thursday, January 8th:

"Georgie and Jack went for a ride. Colonel McKinstry and Marie called and had tea, Marie to say goodbye for some time. Colonel McKinstry brought Mother a present of apples. Eva, Georgie, Hugh and Gustie went to a dance. Mother, Jack, Lil and Mollie stayed at home and played whist."

Friday, January 9th:

"Eva and Georgie came back from the dance, and later Hugh and Gustie. No other news. Lil and Jack drove to Bangor."

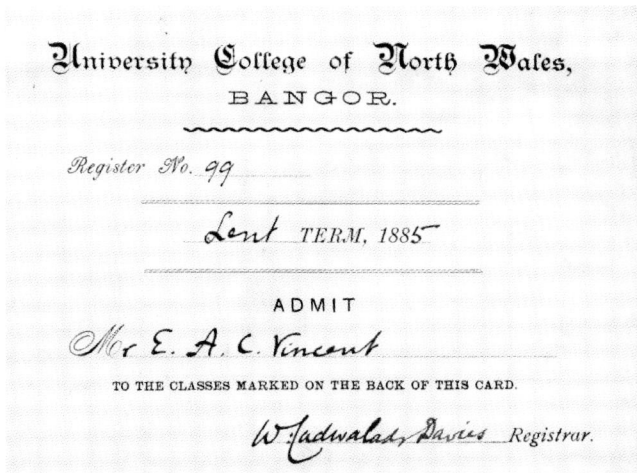

University College of North Wales,
BANGOR.

Register No. 99

Lent TERM, 1885

ADMIT

Mr E. A. C. Vincent

TO THE CLASSES MARKED ON THE BACK OF THIS CARD.

W Jadwalad Davies Registrar.

Saturday, January 10ᵗʰ:

"Eva went to stay at Penrallt [with the Barber family]. Edmund and Gustie went to the College to enrol Gustie."

Sunday, January 11ᵗʰ:

"Mother, Georgie and Mollie had bad colds. Lil, Jack, Hugh and Gustie went to Menai Bridge church."

Monday, January 12ᵗʰ:

"The boys [*Ted, Hugh, Jack and Gustie*] out ferreting all day; shot 25 rabbits and a pheasant. Gustie went to Bangor again about entrance fees to the college. Sent for curtains for drawing room The Sackville-Wests came and brought us books and stayed some time. Katie and Trixie [*Davies*] came in to ask Georgie to go to Treborth Hall but she didn't go because of her cold. The day cold with an east wind."

[Entries for the next three days are in Ted Vincent's hand.]

Tuesday, January 13ᵗʰ:

"Lil and Jack went to Bangor, Jack to see Glyn Williams [*headmaster of Friars' School*], Lil to eat chocolate. Gustie entered the college. Ted went to Bangor to the Wellfield offices [*of Barber and Co., solicitors*]. Mollie in bed for best part of the day. Eva convalescent but cured. Georgie bad".

Wednesday, January 14ᵗʰ:

"JEV [*Ted*] went to Treiorweth on his own invitation. Mollie and Georgie (not fit) also Lil went to the college lecture on English literature [*given by Principal Reichel*]."

Thursday, January 15ᵗʰ:

"JEV returned [*from Anglesey*], went to Carnarvon and came back for dinner. GEV [*Mother*] called at the Canonry. Everyone else did nothing. Whist; whisky; bed".

[Entries for the next three days appear to be in the hand of Lil Vincent.]

Friday, January 16th:

"Mother, Georgie and Jack went to Treborth [*Hall*] to see Trixie and Arthur dressed for a children's fancy dress ball. Trixie was the Evening Star. Lloyd didn't go, felt too old. Weary of the world at 14. Arthur was got up as Jack Frost. Ted went to Assizes at Carnarvon. Lil and Jack went to Bangor."

Saturday, January 17th:

"Hugh and Jack lunched with OE [*Owen Evans*] and brought back Professor Owen of Lampeter to dinner. George and Gus went riding. Ted came back from Carnarvon. A musical at Lime Grove to which no one could go."

[The 'musical' was a meeting of the Amateur Music Society at Lime Grove, Bangor: the programme comprising Haydn and Mozart. Subsequent meetings comprised Schubert and Brahms (Feb. 5th), Handel (Feb. 26th), Chopin, Rubinstein and Grieg (March 5th).]

Sunday, January 18th:

"Mother, Lil, Georgie, Hugh, Gustie and Jack went to the Cathedral at 11.30 and Eva went to the Menai Bridge church."

Monday, January 19th:

"Georgie and Mollie went to lecture. Saw the Davieses' new cart at the station at Bangor, we all got in in turns to try it. Edmund and Hugh went to Carnarvon [*on legal business*]. Charles and Bertie Sackville-West came in the afternoon to watch the boys shoot."

Tuesday, January 20th:

"Jack [*Lloyd- Williams*] went away by the early train [*for his lecturing duties in Lampeter*]. Edmund drove to Beaumaris. Mollie went to Bangor, first to Penrallt to enquire about Mr Barber who had been ill, then on to Lime Grove to see the Sackville-Wests who had bad colds. Mollie stayed there so late that she missed her train and walked back by herself, no adventures [*approximately 4 miles*]."

Wednesday, January 21st:

"Lil, Georgie and Mollie went to lecture and then to luncheon at the Sackville-Wests'. Found them all better."

Thursday, January 22nd:

"Edmund went to Ruthin this morning. Pritchard sent him a 'Brief' as he was starting. Gustie flew with it to Menai Bridge [*railway station*]. Mother and Lil called on Lady Isham and Miss Sandys [*in Menai Bridge town.*] Eva and Mollie went to Bangor and bought Mother a new dolman [*a woman's mantle with cape-like appendages instead of sleeves*]. Lil went to church in the evening. Peggy had a calf. Freezing hard."

Friday, January 23rd:

"Mother and Mollie drove to Bangor and called first on Major and Mrs Fletcher staying at the George Hotel. Then drove on to the Wyatts, afterwards called at Mrs Bulkeley Hughes, Mrs White Griffith, Mrs Whistler, Mrs Richard Pritchard, Mrs Morris Williams, where we had tea. Everyone disappointed about skating, as the ice was not strong enough. Mr Wait [*a friend of Hugh Vincent's and a teacher at Friars' School*] lunched here having come over to skate and being disappointed. Mr Norris Wyatt called, he had on a cherry-coloured waistcoat."

Saturday, January 24th:

"Today saw the account of the battle of Abu Khir [*Abu Klea*], 60 men of ours lost, 800 of the enemy. Lil and Eva went to play tennis at the Rink in the afternoon."

Sunday, January 25th:

"We went to the Cathedral, heard Canon Pryce preach, the anthem good, heard rumours as we were going that the Houses of Parliament had been blown up [*by Irish terrorists*]. Later on we heard more, that the Houses of Parliament, part of Westminster Hall and the White Tower of the Tower of London had been blown up by dynamite. A double guard of men has been sent to watch the [*Menai Strait road and railway*] Bridges. Will gone from London to stay over Sunday with Mr Budworth in Essex." [*Richard Thomas Dutton Budworth was a near contemporary and friend of William Vincent's at Christ College, Brecon. They played cricket together and when Budworth left school in 1886, he joined the Old Breconian team captained by Vincent. Budworth later played rugby for Oxford University and England. He went on to become headmaster of Durham School and a canon of Durham Cathedral.*]

[Entries until February 3rd are by Georgie.]

Monday, January 26ᵗʰ:

"Mollie, Lil and Georgie went to a literature [*lecture*] at the college. Mary and Katie Davies came in to tea with us and told us about their recent visit to Flintshire."

Tuesday, January 27ᵗʰ:

"Eva and Georgie drove into Bangor to do some shopping. Mother and Mollie went to a concert at [*the National School*] Menai Bridge, where they heard Mrs Glanffrwd Thomas sing and Sir Charles Isham play on the piccolo." [*The programme included Thomas Arne's "Where the Bee Sucks" sung by Mrs Glanffrwd Thomas and the Chopin Etudes performed by the Misses Sackville-West.*]

Wednesday, January 28ᵗʰ:

"Mollie, Georgie and Lil went to an examination at the college whereby they were much depressed and did nothing for the rest of the day."

Thursday, January 29ᵗʰ:

"Mollie went to Treiorwerth to see Mary Cotterill [*on a visit home from Edinburgh*] who has been ill and to keep Meg company for a few days."

Friday, January 30ᵗʰ:

"Eva went to Bray [*near Dublin, to visit distantly related 'aunts', Bessie and Fanny Walker, who lived at Glenbrook outside Bray*]. Lil went down to the coverts with Hugh. Georgie had a heavy cold and drank blackcurrant tea."

Saturday, January 31ˢᵗ:

"Lil heard from Mollie, who wanted riding things sent after her [*to Treiorwerth*]. The two last turkeys killed, one sent to Ted and Babs and the other kept at home. Hugh, Georgie and Gustie went to the Rink and enjoyed themselves very much. Georgie played well. A great thunderstorm which came on while they were away alarmed Mother and Lil on their account but they managed to get home without further misfortune. We all who were at home played whist in the evening."

Sunday, February 1ˢᵗ:

"Mother, Lil and Georgie drove to the Cathedral. Hugh and Gus walked. The anthem was 'In the Beginning' and was sung well by the boys but spoilt by the men. Mother heard from Eva in the morning. She arrived safely without being sick, found the aunts all well, Captain Walker flourishing and everybody of course very kind [*Captain Walker was the brother-in-law of Grace Vincent's, brother, Canon William Johnson*]. Mother also heard from Eleanor Edwards who wants to get her boy into Christ's Hospital. She is in trouble, for her husband has gone to South Africa as a missionary. She is to follow him after having found homes for her three children. A letter came from Will, which made us all unhappy. He has not been well and his cough continues — went to a doctor who however doesn't seem to have given at all a bad account of him. He is to come home next Saturday and stay a week."

Monday, February 2nd:

"Mother heard from Ted. Babs has not been well for two days. Ted thinks it was something at a dance which they had been to that made her ill but she is now nearly all right. Georgie, Lil and Gustie went to the college in the afternoon [*to attend the ceremonial opening of the new Physical and Chemical laboratories where the inaugural address was to be given by Sir William Thomson, later Lord Kelvin*]. They enjoyed themselves much but thought they could have done the speeches 'so much better themselves'. Dr Haughton of Dublin was the most amusing speaker. There was an entertainment in the evening to which Gustie alone went as Mother thought it too cold an evening to drive in the dogcart in evening clothes. Gus did not return until midnight."

The new University College of North Wales, with the purpose-built science laboratories on the right. (University of Wales, Bangor)

The Council and Senate of the UNIVERSITY COLLEGE OF
NORTH WALES request the pleasure of the company of

[signature]

at the Ceremony of the Opening of the New Chemical and Physical
Laboratories, on Monday, February 2nd, at 3 p.m. Sir William
Thomson will preside and deliver an Inaugural Address.

A Conversazione will be held at 8 p.m., in the Laboratories.

An early reply addressed to the Principal is requested.

University College,
   Bangor,
      Jan. 21st, 1885.

Tuesday, February 3rd:

"Mother heard from Mr Gurney who does not think Will is looking well. It was a lovely day so Mother and Lil went to call on Mrs Parry of Port-dinorwic [*the vicar's wife*] but only stayed a moment as she and her husband were just starting out. They walked back. Georgie and Hugh walked to Menai Bridge in the vain hope of seeing a gun-boat said to be there for the protection of [*Robert Stephenson's Britannia*] Tubular Bridge but found it not, so have concluded that the boat only existed in [*the groom*] Owen's lively imagination."

Wednesday, February 4th:

"Mollie came home from Treiorwerth. A poor man had been very much hurt in the farmyard by a Traction engine, and there was very little chance of his getting better when she left. On February 3rd as Mollie and Meg Wynne-Jones were driven from Bryngwran, Tom the coachman saw what he took for a ghost. It was a light jumping about as large as the carriage wheel. The horse saw it too and was frightened and then it disappeared. Hugh ran with the Marquis' Beagles yesterday and was a good deal tired."

H. Vincent.

THE
MARQUIS OF ANGLESEY'S

GASCOGNE   HOUNDS

WILL MEET

Monday

Tuesday

Wednesday *Feb 4th Cefu du Saf*

Thursday

Friday

Saturday *Feb 7th Lyn y Caeau*

at *12* o'clock.

Thursday, February 5th:

"Heard from Eva, she seems to be getting better. Lil and Mollie went to luncheon at Lime Grove where they practised [*for the Amateur Musical Society meeting that evening which comprised Schubert and Brahms*], missed a lecture which they were sorry for. Mother and Hugh came later in the afternoon. The musical not as good as usual. Lil and Mollie saw a telegram in the North Wales Chronicle office 'Kartoum taken by treachery. General Gordon probably taken prisoner'. This is supposed to be an official telegram from Lord Wolseley.

The Chief Constable from Carnarvon here today looking after the guarding of the Tube [*the Britannia Railway Bridge*]. The officials have been warned that it is to be blown up between 5 and 7 tomorrow. There was a company of soldiers sent to Holyhead and there are policemen stationed everywhere but still no one really believes it will happen. Old Miss Sandys of Menai Bridge was married the other day. She is over 60, and the man she has married is 73. 8 p.m.: 5 shots heard down at the Tube."

Friday, February 6th:

"The Tube was not blown up today. The news from Kartoum confirmed, but no details yet known. Every sort of conjecture is made about Gordon's fate and preparations are being made for sending more troops out."

Saturday, February 7th:

"Our [*tennis*] day at the Rink. Mother and Georgie drove and Mollie and Lil by train. Hugh and Gustie walked in later. Mollie and Georgie chose a hat for Lil. It was a fine day so it all looked bright: the party we had invited were 3 Sackville-Wests, 2 Wyatts, 1 Barber, 1 Hughes, Mr Wait, Mr Trechmann, Miss Bulkeley Hughes. The tea was very good and it all passed off very well. Everyone talked of Gordon and Kartoum and nothing else. No fresh news from Egypt yet."

Sunday, February 8th:

"It rained without stopping all day and blew hard, no one went to church except Lil in the evening, the whole family read Scott's novels all day. Norah paid us a short visit, as she found she could spare half an hour from her puppies."

Monday, February 9th:

"Heard from Eva [*in Ireland*], she says she is better. Worked and tried to mark out pattern on new drawing room curtains with Katie [*Davies's*] help but it was a miserable failure. Mrs Griffith Williams and Mary Macgillycuddy appeared after luncheon and stayed all afternoon."

Tuesday, February 10th:

"The last day given to the Tube and it looks like a rock. Today Lil and Mollie began the drawing room curtains. Lil and Hugh went for a walk in the cover. Mollie and Georgie went for a walk also in the cover — they got catkins and willow buds, and came back and made bouquets with them and snowdrops. Sent some to Babs and Ted. Mother read the account of troops going out to Egypt. Did some more work, read, bed. Rain at intervals all day. Will coming home [*from London*] tomorrow."

Wednesday, February 11th:

"Went to lecture this morning — had our papers given back, not bad marks. Mr Wait came to tea and dinner, he and Mother and Georgie went to walk in the lower park. Lil and Mollie went to Menai Bridge. Will came home at half past eight, not looking very well."

Thursday, February 12th:

"Georgie and Mollie went to Bangor, walked back. Will looking better, out all day. After luncheon new oil cloth put on stairs. Mrs Bulkeley Hughes and her daughter spent the afternoon here. News came today of the death of General Earle. [*Major-General William Earle, commanding the force sent to relieve Khartoum, was shot in action on February 10th.*] Yesterday news of Gordon's death made certain. He was stabbed on the 25th of January at Kartoum. Lil went to church. Will told stories of 3 Powis Square [*where he lived in London, preparing for ICS entry*]."

Friday, February 13th:

"Unpleasant day as 13ths always are."

Saturday, February 14th:

"Valentine's Day. Came to Treborth that day 1878. Hugh and Gustie had 2 Valentines but have not discovered the senders. Hugh's was a potato cut into a rose with some lines of indifferent poetry. Hugh and Gustie ran with the Marquis' hounds, they had a good day of exercise but not good sport. Lionel Sackville-West lunched here. Lil and Georgie went to Carnarvon. Sent a wreath of snowdrops and moss to London to the Charles Joneses [*Mrs Charles Jones having died on February 11th*]."

Sunday, February 15th:

"Lil, Georgie and Mollie went to the Cathedral this morning, a special prayer was read for the troops going out to Egypt. Letter from Eva."

Monday, February 16th:

"Lil, Georgie and Mollie went to Bangor, first to Madame Lazarus about dresses and then on to the college, where they had a very poor and short lecture … and then … a beastly paper to do which they did badly. Came home, beastly east wind with fog. Mollie went to tea at Treborth Hall. Evening as usual. Norah yelled in the night and had not only to be let out of the house but had to be accompanied by the delicate Mollie to the stables where her puppies live … the hour was two, the night dark, wet 'and all alone went she'. She came back also not improved in temper."

Ash Wednesday, February 18th:

"Mother, Will and Mollie went to the [*Menai*] Bridge church. Weather as usual on Ash Wednesday, cold and bright. Will went back to London by the 3 o'clock train. Mary Macgillycuddy came here to stay until Monday."

Thursday, February 19th:

"Lil, Georgie and Mollie went to lecture in the afternoon, had their papers back. Pretty well marked: Mrs Verney 21; next marked to hers 17; MMV [*Mollie*] 14, EACV [*Lil*] 12, GGV [*Georgie*] 7 for only one question (everyone else did 2). Hugh drove Mary Macgillycuddy over in the dogcart and they two and Mollie went to tea at the Wyatts'. Today was a hard frost."

Friday, February 20th:

"Freezing hard, went for a walk with Mary Mac. Cecilie Sackville-West and Mr Owen Evans came and brought Eva and Mollie the little book in memorial of the Dean, which they were very glad to have." [*The Dean in question was the recently deceased Very Reverend H.T. Edwards, who had been greatly loved. He had been the immediate successor of James Crawley Vincent as Vicar of Caernarfon in 1869, and of James V. Vincent as Dean of Bangor in 1876.*]

Saturday, February 21st:

"Still freezing and dreadfully cold. Mollie and Mary Macgillycuddy drove into Bangor to the Rink, Hugh and Gus went to run with the hounds but the scent wouldn't lie and the hounds couldn't do anything — they were both a good deal disappointed. Georgie had Trixie and Arthur to tea and Arthur distinguished himself by eating 17 sponge cakes. Mary and Cecilie Sackville-West gave us a big basket of snowdrops."

Sunday, February 22nd:

"Raining and windy, most of the family not devout. Mollie heard from Ted this morning and he sent a copy of his book on football [*the first history of the game ever written*], Ted and Babs asked Georgie and Mollie to go up to London, which they hope to do after lectures are over."

Wednesday, February 25th:

"Beautiful day, almost spring. Lil, Georgie and Mollie drove to lecture, Mollie went to luncheon at Lime Grove and went a long walk with Cecilie Sackville-West over the hill, mountains more wonderful than usual. Mother, Lil and George went to the [*Menai*] Bridge station, bought a copy of *Rasselas* [*by Samuel Johnson*] and a life of Gordon."

Friday, February 27th:

"Went to church at Menai Bridge. Lil and Gustie went to Treborth Hall to tea … Gustie breakfasted at the college [*with Principal Reichel*]. Gus spoke at the college debating society on Pitt. Lionel Sackville-West spoke too."

Saturday, February 28th:

"Mary Evans and Mollie went to Bangor and had tea with Mr Owen Evans at Cliff Cottage. Day most lovely. Went to service, came out before the service was done."

St David's Day, Sunday, March 1st:

"Walked to the Cathedral. Mother and Gus walked across the [*Menai Suspension*] bridge with the Fletchers. Day very fine again, everyone very tired."

Monday, March 2nd:

"Rained. Lil and Georgie to Portdinorwic … Mary and Lionel Sackville-West came and spent the afternoon, Mr Owen Evans came to dinner, we had music and whist, Georgie and Mollie planted primroses — Georgie planted, Mollie looked on. Sent Ted some flower roots."

Tuesday, March 3rd:

"Very wet day. Georgie and Mollie and Trixie went down to the cover, got dirty, [*collected*] primrose roots and found Bishop's caps out. Came up and had tea. Sir Charles and Lady Isham tooled over in a very small pony carriage with a self-willed pony. They stood out in the rain some time, apparently not in any way affected by the weather. Sir Charles was rather more like 'the old party of Prague' than usual. Eva at Treiorwerth."

Wednesday, March 4th:

"War news very bad. Australian contingent started [*embarked*]. Lil, Georgie and Mollie went to lecture this morning …. Hugh as usual poking over tennis ground. Norris Wyatt came, looked as usual very nice, and like a big robin in his red waistcoat. Parry BA [*vicar of Llanfair-is-gaer, Portdinorwic*] and his wife came and a pupil in a wig. The wig does not break the fourth commandment. Georgie and Mollie planted a lot of primroses. Captain Morgan sent game — wild duck, snipe." [*Captain Francis F.R. Mansel Morgan, J.P., D.L., lived at Plas Coed Mor on the Anglesey side of the Menai Strait, close to the Britannia Bridge and virtually opposite Treborth Uchaf.*]

Thursday, March 5th:

"Mr Reichel and Cecilie Sackville-West came to luncheon. The day particularly wet and cold — luncheon passed off well. Mr Reichel stiff in manner but means well one hopes. Major and Mrs Fletcher asked but did not come to luncheon. Major Fletcher came later on and admired the filly very much. Mary Evans went to Carnarvon by 5 o'clock train. Mary and Edith Davies came in for a short time — we all felt tired after so many visitors and were very glad to think that we had the house for once to ourselves."

Friday, March 6th:

Lil, Georgie and Mollie went to the college in the afternoon, Mr Reichel lectured on Sheridan and Burns. They went first to the Cathedral, rather quick service read by Mr Owen Evans. Had an examination paper at the college. Went back to the Davieses' [*Treborth Hall*] to tea. In the morning Mollie had planted some anemone seeds or roots sent her by Ted, also had Japanese primroses planted. Owen [*the groom*] showed her a splendid Tobacco-case which had been sent him from 'the foreign'."

Saturday, March 7th:

"A beautiful day, mountains covered with snow, sun quite warm, sky blue. Miss Barber and Miss Harriet Williams called in the morning, neither of them were brilliant in conversation. Mollie and Georgie drove to the Rink — the Wyatts' day. They had some good sets. Lil had Arthur and Trixie in to tea, when M and G came home Hugh was making them 'Jacky lanterns' out of turnips and Arthur was eating as usual. Hugh ran with the Marquis' hounds — they met at Plas Llanfair [*home of the Marquis of Anglesey's estate manager*]. Gustie went to play a football match between the college and Beaumaris which the college won. The troops in Egypt have taken up Summer quarters and sent for a pack of hounds so it may be concluded there will be no more prayers for them just at present."

Sunday, March 8th:

"Wet day, stayed at home. Lil and Mollie went to the 'Tin' in the evening." [*The 'Tin' was the small church nearest to Treborth Uchaf in Penrhosgarnedd: at the time it had an iron frame and corrugated roof, and was extremely noisy during rain and hail. Lil often played the harmonium for services there.*]

Monday, March 9th:

"Went to the college in the morning. Georgie and Mollie went to Portdinorwic to have jackets tried on. Miss Wyatt brought some double snowdrop roots."

Tuesday, March 10th:

"Mollie and Hugh drove to the Sackville Wests for luncheon, jolly day but cold. Went to the Rink, had some very good games, everyone almost being decent players. People there: 2 Miss Vaughans — nieces of Lady Isham, Mr Reichel, Mr Thomson. Stayed too late and had to drive from Bangor in less than 20 minutes. Drove to the Canonry with the Davies party — sacred music and few men, music decent taken all round and the whole thing well managed. The drives there and back decidedly fun. Mollie and Lil's duet a success."

Wednesday, March 11th:

"Went to the college in the morning. Mary Davies came in and talked over the party of the night before. Mollie took Georgie and Lil to tennis."

Thursday, March 12th:

"Mother and Mollie walked to the Ishams to luncheon. Mother on her way home called on Mrs Norman (née Sandys) but heard her say [*presumably to the maid*] she was out. Mollie went to see Mrs John Davies [*daughter-in-law of Richard Davies of Treborth Hall*]. Mollie went to Treborth, had some tennis, Georgie and Hugh did ditto. Will Wynne Jones [*vicar of Caernarfon, son of Mrs Grace Vincent's first cousin, the Archdeacon of Bangor, the Ven. J.W. Wynne-Jones*] came from Carnarvon and dined here. Robert Monteith sent violets from France."

Friday, March 13th:

"Blue day as usual — Mollie went to Portdinorwic. Mother, Georgie and Mollie went to Bangor to the commemoration service [*in Bangor Cathedral, in remembrance of General Gordon and others who died*]. The Bishop gave the address, he looks very ill and the address was dull. The best part of the service was the Dead March which was as usual. In the afternoon a cram of visitors to tea — 5 Ishams, 2 Pryces. Mollie went to Mrs White Griffith's to tea, talked spiritualism which appears interesting nonsense. Evening tiresome, in fact a 13th day. Hugh had tea with Mr Wait and called on 2 Professors, we don't like Professors — they have nasty clothes, big noses, squeaky voices, spectacles, bad manners."

BANGOR CATHEDRAL.

A COMMEMORATIVE SERVICE

WILL BE HELD

IN THIS CATHEDRAL,

On FRIDAY NEXT, MARCH 13th,

AT II A.M.

IN REMEMBRANCE OF GENERAL GORDON, AND OTHERS WHO HAVE FALLEN.

ORDER OF SERVICE.

1. The Burial Service, to the end of the Lesson.

2. Address.

3. The Burial Service resumed at the Anthem, " I heard a voice," to the end of the last Collect.

4. Four Intercessions from the Litany, viz. :—

We beseech Thee to hear us, O Lord God, and that it may please Thee to succour, help, and comfort, all that are in danger, necessity, and tribulation :

We beseech Thee to hear us, good Lord.

That it may please Thee to preserve all that travel by land, or by water, all women labouring of child, all sick persons, and young children ; and to shew thy pity upon all prisoners and captives ;

We beseech Thee to hear us, good Lord.

That it may please Thee to defend, and provide for, the fatherless children, and widows, and all that are desolate and oppressed ;

We beseech Thee to hear us, good Lord

That it may please Thee to have mercy upon all men ;

We beseech Thee to hear us, good Lord.

Collects in time of War.

Brief Silence.

5. Benediction.

BANGOR, MARCH 7TH, 1885.

Friday, March 27ᵗʰ:

"Will came home looking all right. Lent term ended well for Gus at the college. Ted and Babs are well and we are all the rest of us at home."

Palm Sunday, March 29ᵗʰ:

"Will Wynne-Jones inducted at Llanbeblig [*Caernarfon*]. The day was wet and stormy. The Archdeacon [*Will Wynne-Jones' father*] went over for it to Carnarvon. John Davies' little baby (little Jack) died. He had only lived a fortnight."

Easter Day, April 5ᵗʰ:

"Mother and Mollie drove to Carnarvon, went to Llanbeblig [*church*]. The militia as usual and the day bright but cold. Will Wynne preached. Eva and Will went to Menai Bridge [*church*], the rest to the Cathedral."

Easter Monday, April 6ᵗʰ:

"Hugh gone for the day in the mountains with the Sackville-Wests. Will and Gus to the last run of the Marquis' hounds. Lil, George and Mollie went down to the cover — found Mollie's cow ill, great excitement as no man was to be found. Mother and Old Owen poured down gruel and whiskey with a horn and it was better. The trainer brought in the filly after keeping her out many hours, he was drunk, very. Lain on the corn-chest and refused counsel. The evening passed in moralising on the sins of others."

[*There then follows a description by Hugh Vincent of his day in the mountains.*]

"Hugh went with the Sackville-Wests over, no, not over but half way up the Glyders. They started from Lime Grove in Robin Cric's break, driving unicorn. [*'Cric' was H.R. Clegg of Plas Llanfair, estate manager to the Marquis of Anglesey. 'Driving unicorn' meant driving three horses: two abreast and one leader.*] The party consisted of Colonel Sackville-West, Miss Sackville-West, Cecilie Sackville-West, Lionel, Charlie and Bertie Sackville-West, Miss Rathbone, Prof. Gray [*Professor of Physics*] of the North Wales College, also Prof. Roberts [*Professor of Greek*], Owen Evans, Miss Evans, Mrs Foulkes Jones and Hugh. On the way Robin Cric discoursed with Hugh and Lionel who were sitting on the box on the delights of driving and on the beauty and science of his own more particularly. Having arrived at Ogwen, Colonel Sackville-West, Miss Sackville-West , Lionel, Bertie and Charlie, Owen Evans [*and*] the two profs were 'disembogued' from the break leaving the others to drive round to Penygwryd to meet them after their intended ascent of the Glyders. They started gaily enough and got as far as [*Lake*] Bochlwyd with immense success, the only drawback being that Charlie had to go back as he was not very well. At this point their troubles began. Imagine going over huge boulders covered deep with snow, carefully poking about first with a stick before putting your foot down. However, on they struggled manfully, over boulders, up steep, slippery inclines on hands and knees and sometimes crawling on, well, parts that were not intended to crawl upon in nature's original design. Lionel and Hugh got about 100 yards in front of the others. Twice they thought it would be absolutely impossible to get on but eventually succeeded and struggled further on. At last they came to a point within about 30 yards of the top where victory so to speak was almost in their grasp, where it became quite hopeless to attempt any further advance. Sheer rocks rising straight and menacing on both sides of them covered with half thawed ice. In vain they attempted to get a footing: there was nothing to get any hold of. Here then they came to a stop and watched the rest of the party struggling up. Almost the first sight that met them was the unfortunate little Prof. Roberts tumbling head over heels in the snow down the hill. He had missed his footing and down he went, like a tee-to-tum for about a hundred yards. It was really a rather appalling sight. However, they were all much relieved by hearing a rather doleful little voice echoing up the rocks assuring them that he was not badly hurt. By this time Lionel and Hugh began to descend and when they had come down to the rest of the party, after a brief consultation, it was unanimously decided that the attempt must be given up and the descent begun. The only difficulty was how it was to be done; and the only feasible plan was to 'slither'. So they began; Hugh first squatted down in the snow and slid merrily along to the first place where he could get a good footing. Then came Prof. Roberts, who by the way had mounted up to the others; again the miserable little man came to smash. Instead of sliding straight down to the spot where Hugh was waiting to receive him, he shot off to one side and over the edge of a small precipice on his head. However, he came down luckily on a good heap of soft snow and was not hurt. Then came Colonel Sackville-West who reached Hugh with success and waited with him for the next comer. Miss West then came slithering down, but shot past both Colonel Sackville-West and Hugh but luckily arrived at a fairly safe place. Then came Bertie who was just stopped by Hugh. Then Owen Evans muttering loud and deep prayers came tumbling down head over heels and might really have been hurt but being large and heavy stopped at last by his own weight some way below the others. Then came Miss Rathbone whose descent I will pass over in silence; suffice it to say, it was more successful than graceful. Lastly Lionel came sliding down, as cool as a cucumber looking rather as if he were driving a tandem with a puny leader who required some management. Thus they all arrived without any broken bones at the bottom. Nothing could possibly describe the scene either of ascent or descent, there was such a mixture of comedy and tragedy in it. Miss Sackville-West and Miss Rathbone deserve peculiar credit for their behaviour all through the extraordinary performance. On their arrival at the bottom, Hugh and Lionel walked round to Penygwryd by Capel Curig and told the story to the party there who were feeling rather uneasy. They then started back towards home in the break and picking up the rest of the party at Capel Curig, arrived safely home after their day's adventure."

[*The entry for Easter Monday is completed by William Vincent's record of his participation, together with his brother Gustie, in the final meet of the season of the Marquis of Anglesey's Hounds. The gentlemen ran, the ladies rode.*]

"Gus and Will went to Llanfair to the final meet of the Marquis of Anglesey's hounds for the season. It was partly intended as a show-meet and there were crowds of people to see us start. Mrs Roberts of Rhiwlas and the 2 Miss Gartsides appeared on horseback. H.R. Griffith and Colonel Griffith were there in knickers, otherwise the people seemed got up for show rather than running. H.R. Clegg [*of Plas Llanfair*] gave a nice hunting breakfast; Will and Gus went in but did not eat anything; in fact no one did seem to eat anything. The "Princess" [*presumably Clegg's daughter*] was inside looking very pretty … After loitering about an hour at Plas Llanfair the Marquis led off the hounds towards Menai Bridge and then up away from the sea. After drawing one or two fields, the hounds found a ploughed field and went away. Some of the less cunning runners went off at full pace across the soft plough, but the more wary took the side and were content to walk. At the end of the field the running really began and the bob-tail was left behind in the ploughed land. After about thirty minutes' hard going including one or two stiff water jumps, there was a check on a gorse bank. At this point the Marquis appeared about 3 fields off and called back the hounds.

However, they had to return to the gorse bank, where in about 10 minutes they clued again and went away fast. About a mile further along there was another check and the hounds found they had overrun the hare. The Marquis called back the hounds again and they found [*the scent*] in about 5 minutes and were off again. Both Gus and Will were here left behind and only arrived to find the hounds checked again and the Marquis thinking of giving up the chase. As the search was rather hopeless the Marquis gathered his hounds and we started home. After a bad attempt at a cut across country, Gillart picked up both the boys and drove them very kindly to the bridge, whence after a short visit to the "Antelope" [*public house*] they walked on and arrived at Treborth rather tired at about 5 p.m."

Tuesday, April 7th:

"Gustie went to see a football match at Bangor. Edith and Katie came in to settle about the photo in caps and gowns. The Prince and Princess of Wales passed through on their way [*to Ireland*], the boys and Lil went down to the Tube to see the train pass."

Wednesday, April 8th:

"Will went back to London. Cecilie and Bertie Sackville-West came to see us. Charlie in bed. Mary Evans and O.E. [*Owen Evans*] to dinner, day more or less wearisome."

Thursday, April 9th:

"Finished and put up two pairs of the drawing room curtains. Mr Shipley came in the evening, also Uncle William and Vincent Johnson unexpectedly; they stayed the night." [*Conway Shipley was a family friend who had been at Christ Church with Ted. He taught at Dulwich College, London. 'Uncle William' was the younger Reverend William Johnson, brother of Mrs Grace Vincent. His youngest son, Vincent, was then aged 13.*]

Friday, April 10th:

"Mr Owen Williams spent part of this day here, he was very amusing, particularly playing Whist with Mother and Mr Shipley. Mollie's cow died. Mollie, Lil, Edith and Georgie photographed at Treborth in caps and gowns."

Saturday, April 11th:

"Mr Owen Williams went away at 12. Mr Shipley, Hugh and Mollie drove to the Rink; it was rather dull."

Sunday, April 12th:

"Went to the Cathedral, slept, wrote letters, read novels, smoked, had tea. Georgie and Mr Shipley went to Menai Bridge to post letters. Mollie, Lil and Hugh to Penrhos church to 'halloring Anthems'."

Monday, April 13th:

"Mother, Mollie and Mr Shipley went to tea at the Rathbones', the gardens were crammed full of flowers. Edmund coming home. Gustie's little dog arrived."

Tuesday, April 14th:

"Edmund arrived at 4 a.m. Hugh and Edmund to Carnarvon. Lil, Georgie and Mr Shipley walked around Nant-y-Garth, Mollie spent the afternoon at Lime Grove, missed her train, walked home. Edmund brought back Ebin Edwards to dinner, the Davieses came in afterwards and Katie sang very well. Good day taken all round."

Wednesday, April 15th:

"Mr Shipley went away at half past eight. Mrs Richard Davies [*of Treborth Hall*] came in to say goodbye before going to London. Mrs John Davies drove round with her. Mary [*Davies*] came in too. Visitors all afternoon. Ted and Hugh at Carnarvon. Mr Wait spent a long evening here. We all went to bed tired out with social exertions. Mollie tried out the filly (Dian) for the first time, went well and quietly."

Thursday, April 16th:

"Wet day, finished the last two curtains. Went to tea at the Davieses. Edmund had a 'brief' in Carnarvon. Jack Lloyd-Williams and [*his sister*] Kate Williams arrived at half past six."

Friday, April 17th:

"Edmund went to Chester by the six o'clock train this morning. Best spring day we have yet had. Mollie and Georgie rode in the afternoon, Hugh went to Bangor, Jack and Lil invisible, Eva and Kate Williams to the bridge. No visitors. Mollie and Georgie saw men out with guns and dogs, apparently coursing, but why guns and the wrong time of year. Mother has 2 sad little chickens out. The Davieses all went to London this morning."

Saturday, April 18th:

"Beautiful day. Lil, Jack, Kate and Georgie drove to the Monument [*the Marquis of Anglesey's Column in Llanfairpwll*]. Mrs Will Wynne Jones came to call and brought [*her daughter*] Margaret dressed all in blue like a forget-me-not, she is a very pretty and nice little child. Mr Charles Jones came at 5, sang very well in the evening and was very nice. Mother and Mollie saw a red admiral butterfly for the first time this year."

Sunday, April 19th, Primrose Day:

"Went to the Cathedral, Mr Charles Jones sang the litany. Hugh and Gus walked up the Glyder and threw snowballs at each other, the day was very warm down here. Eva alone went to evening service. Many people in the Cathedral wore primroses."

Monday, April 20th:

"Georgie saw the first swallow. Mr Charles Jones went away that morning."

Tuesday, April 21st:

"Hugh went up to London by the early train."

Wednesday, April 22nd:

"Gus found 3 pheasant nests. Mr Charles Jones came back again. Music and whist. Mollie saw 4 wild geese fly across to Vaynol." [*Vaynol was the house of the Assheton-Smith family, set in a large area of elegantly landscaped park and woodland, immediately to the south-west of Treborth Uchaf, and bordering the Menai Strait.*]

Thursday, April 23rd:

"Lil, Jack, Kate and Georgie went to Beaumaris, had tea at the Thomases' and saw the castle. [*Madge Thomas and her brother William were distant cousins of the Vincents. He was a retired lieutenant-colonel and Chief Constable of Anglesey.*] Mollie went to see Mrs John Davies at Treborth [*Mrs Grace Elizabeth Davies, née Habershon of London had married John Davies in 1883. Her brother, Dr S.H. Habershon, later married Katie Davies*]. Mrs Norman called — fine day, whist."

Saturday, April 25th:

"Lil, Jack, Kate and Gus went up Snowdon, the wind was very high and they had a good deal of rain. Georgie and Mollie went to the Rink. Eleven goslings came out."

Sunday, April 26th:

"Went to the Cathedral in the morning. Lil, Eva and Georgie to evening service at the 'Tin'."

Monday, April 27th:

"Hugh's birthday, he is still in London. Johnnie Evans and Mr Henry Williams spent the day here, Mrs Rathbone came and bought Lil's cow. Heard the cuckoo for the first time."

Tuesday, April 28th:

"Hugh came down from London where he had enjoyed himself very much: had been to see the Davieses and Charles Jones; dined with Mr Shipley; dined at the Constitutional Club; was asked to dine with Mr Ebin Edwards at the 'Junior Carlton', and had seen *The Private Secretary* [*by Charles Hawtrey at the Globe Theatre*]. Hugh bought a very tall new hat and had been asked to go to a dance with the Ramsays." [*Although Sir Andrew Ramsay had retired as Director of the Geological Survey of Great Britain, he and Lady Louisa were continuing to live in both London and Beaumaris.*]

Wednesday, April 29th:

"Meg Wynne-Jones and Cecilie [*Sackville-West*] called in the morning. Started for Gorddinog at half past six, all felt rather dreary driving in evening clothes through the daylight, spirits revived when we got to Gorddinog. [*They were attending an 'At Home with Theatricals and Dancing' at Gorddinog, the house in Llanfairfechan in which their father had grown up. It was now owned by Colonel and Mrs Henry Platt. The evening included a performance of* Old Soldiers *by H.J. Byron, a popular writer of burlesques, who had died the previous year.*] The play very good for amateurs and the room very jolly, the house as usual very jolly, loads of flowers everywhere and primroses everywhere they could be put. The relations of the family were there in force: 2 Wynne-Jones, (Meg and Bob) [*Robert Iorwerth Wynne-Jones and his sister Georgina Margaret*]; Edward Birley; Mr Roland Williams; Colonel Thomas; Cousin Madge and Mr Hugh Thomas. The dancing was kept up until half past two, heard the corncrake as we were coming home."

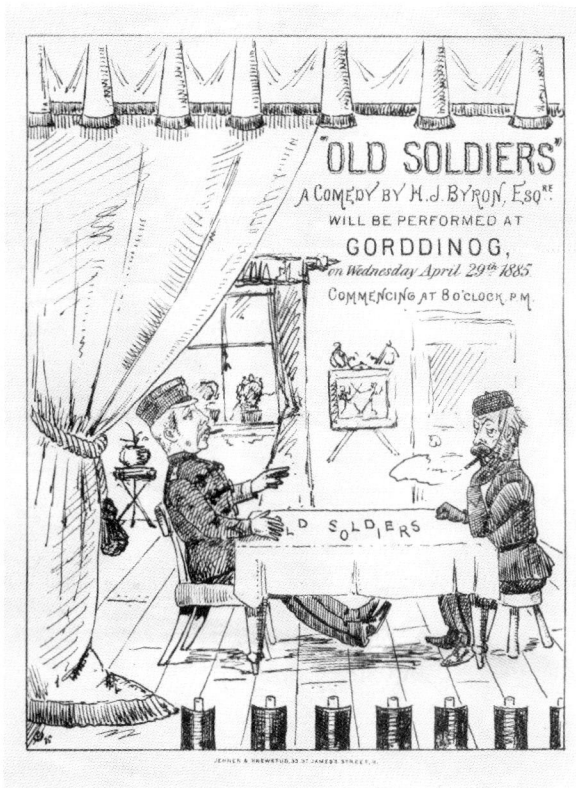

Thursday, April 30th:

"Got up late. Jack went away. Lil, Georgie and Kate Williams tired after the day spent at Conway and Llandudno. Hugh and Mollie drove to Carnarvon to see Jessie Wynne-Jones, found that she had got the [*vicarage*] dining room into order and that it looked very well. [*The Hon. Jessie Wynne-Jones, daughter of Lord Aberdare, was married to the vicar, their second cousin Will. The Llanbeblig, Caernarfon vicarage was the house in which the six younger Vincent children had been born.*]

Mr Reichel and Mr Arnold called here and had tea." [*Edward V. Arnold was the Professor of Latin at the University College in Bangor.*]

Friday, May 1st:

"Lil, Kate Williams and Gustie went to Carnarvon to see *Old Soldiers* again acted for the benefit of the Life-boat. Eva found a large mushroom."

Saturday, May 2nd:

"Mollie and Hugh went for a ride. Kate Williams, Lil and Mollie went to a musical at the Canonry."

Sunday, May 3rd:

"Went to the Cathedral in the morning."

Monday, May 4th:

"Rained all day. Eleanor Edwards lunched and spent the afternoon here."

Tuesday, May 5th:

"Mr King came from Ireland at 5.05. [*Robert MacFarland King was a Trinity College contemporary of Hugh Vincent. They had played rugby together for the College.*] Hugh and Mollie went for a ride. Hugh dined at the Militia Mess at Carnarvon. New carpet in Eva's room. Played whist in the evening."

Wednesday, May 6th:

"Very cold day, snow again on the mountains. Hugh and Mr King walked to Bangor, Dora Watkin-Davies spent an hour here on her way home from Ruabon. Hugh and Mr King drove her to Menai Bridge."

Thursday, May 7th:

"Mr and Miss Arnold came to tea, also Jane Hughes. Jane Hughes sang. It was a dull party."

Friday, May 8th:

"Cold day. Eva, Georgie, Mr King and Hugh went to Carnarvon to play tennis. Hugh and Mr King went to Mr Fairchild's house to tea, Eva and Georgie to the vicarage. Mary Sackville-West and Charlie came and spent the afternoon."

Saturday, May 9th:

"The Pennants [*the family of Lord Penrhyn*] came in the morning and forced Mollie to be secretary for the LHMA [*Ladies' Home Mission Association*] much against her will. Mother went to Treiorwerth until Monday. Kate Williams and Mr King and Mollie went to play tennis at Penrhyn with the Sackville-Wests. It rained a good deal and blew but the day was a success. They all enjoyed themselves very much. Lil, Eva and Georgie did no particular mischief that day. Played rhyming game in the evening." [*A newspaper cutting reports that on this day Gustie scored 40 runs for Bangor in a cricket match against Friars' School.*]

Sunday, May 10th:

"Went to Cathedral in the morning, very cold day."

Monday, May 11th:

"Mother still at Treiorwerth. Hugh and Mr King went to Carnarvon to play tennis, dined with Mr Humfreys."

Tuesday, May 12th:

"Mother came back from Treiorwerth."

Wednesday, May 13th:

"Lovely day. Jin Marshall came to luncheon, she is nice and pretty, spent the day in walking about and playing tennis against the side of the house."

Ascension Day, Thursday, May 14th:

"Mollie drove all about Bangor with Cecilie, bought a dress for Lil. Mollie tried to find out about the secretary business for the LHMA. Cecilie came back to tea. Lil, Kate and Georgie to tea with the Miss Mousedales." [*The Moulsedales, Mary, 52 and Margaret, 51, who lived at 4 Menai Ville Terrace, Menai Bridge, were daughters of a clerical family with Anglesey connections and were long-standing friends of Grace Vincent.*]

Friday, May 15th:

"Mr King and Hugh out walking. Hugh dined with the Militia officers that evening, drove home, cold wet night."

Saturday, May 16th:

"Cold day and wet in the morning, Mr King, Hugh and Mollie met the Sackville-Wests at Menai Bridge, and drove in Robin Cric's break to Newborough [*in south Anglesey*], when the whole party walked across the sand to Llanddwyn, about 3 miles. Saw the abbey, had learned remarks by Frank Barber, who was got up in riding trousers, reason unknown, having spread the cloth with a brisk wind blowing, requiring it to have many stones put to keep the cloth in place. A drenching shower after we had served the food under ulsters [*a style of overcoat*] and umbrellas. The rain having stopped, the party ate a great deal of salmon and apricot jam. Went about rocks, looked at the sea and came back over the sand to Newborough, and drove home. Saw the new moon, and wished at all the crossroads and got home at half past ten. Gustie made a score of 17 against Beaumaris for Bangor."

Sunday, May 17th:

"Went to Cathedral, cold day."

Monday, May 18th:

"Cold day, Mr King goes away today. We all say au revoir and not goodbye."

Tuesday, May 19th:

"Hugh went to Treiorwerth for rook shooting."

Wednesday, May 20th:

"Grace came to see us. Eva and Mollie went to tea with Mrs White Griffith. John Davies came to dinner. Hugh came back from Treiorwerth with lots of young rooks."

Thursday, May 21st:

"Georgie's birthday. Numerous small presents and a silver locket and chain from Mr King. In the morning Meg Wynne-Jones came from Treiorwerth and then Mollie, Hugh and Gustie went to Carnarvon to see the new colours given to the regiment. Arrived too late, but saw the whole body march past. Went up to the vicarage, had tea and saw Bob Wynne-Jones who arrived while they were there. [*Robert Iorwerth Wynne-Jones was the younger brother, pursuing a brewing career in Scotland.*] Came home, dressed for the ball and started off. [*They were attending, at the invitation of Lieutenant-Colonel Platt and the Officers of the Fourth Battalion of the Royal Welch Fusiliers, a regimental ball at the Sportsman Hotel, Caernarfon.*] A great many people there, lots of officers and their red coats made the whole room look pretty, floor good, music good, company indifferent, Eva enjoyed herself very much, Mollie and Hugh not at all, Mother very sleepy, got home at 5 o'clock."

Friday, May 22nd:

"Meg, Will and Bob Wynne-Jones came to luncheon after which Will, Bob and Hugh played pitch-and-toss, proceeds given to Carnarvon Christ Church spire. [*Christ Church was built by the Rev. James Crawley Vincent. The east window was subscribed as a memorial to the former vicar and the church spire was added during the incumbency of Will Wynne-Jones.*] Meg drove to the station [*Menai Bridge*] to get a 5 o'clock train. Will went to Carnarvon at 5.05. Colonel McKinstry called, told us 'home truths'."

Saturday, May 23rd:

"Jack arrived at 12 o'clock. Day cold and wet."

Whit-Sunday, May 24th:

"Most of the family went to the Cathedral, all except Mollie and Georgie who had colds."

Whit-Monday, May 25th:

"Jack and Kate Williams went away by the early train. Lil went with the Wests up the Glyders and enjoyed herself very much and caught a cold. Mr Wait lunched here, and told us he was going away from Friars' [*School*] at the end of term. Mr Thomas the curate from Bodedern came and stayed some time, servants out for a holiday, general discomfort."

Tuesday, May 26th:

"Gustie went to play tennis at Lime Grove. Everyone still has colds, a day without visitors."

Wednesday, May 27th:

"New cook arrived from Bodedern. Gustie to play tennis at the Wyatts'. Telegram from Will to say he was coming home tonight."

Thursday, May 28th:

"Mr Thomas of Bodedern came to luncheon, Mary Sackville-West and May Edwards came to luncheon too, stayed until 6. Cold day and windy. May Edwards looks very nice and is pretty."

Friday, May 29th, Oak Day:

"Awful wind all day. Mrs Arthur Darbyshire to luncheon. [*The Darbyshire family were prominent in the North Wales quarrying industry. Arthur Darbyshire, JP, owned the Pen-yr-Orsedd Slate Quarries in the Nantlle valley.*] Will and Georgie went to tennis at the Sackville-Wests'. Eva and Mollie went to a school feast at Penrhos, rather fun and the children did eat."

Saturday, May 30th:

"Eva and Georgie went to the Wyatts' to tennis, found it dull. Will and Gus to play cricket. Meg came to see us on her way from Beaumaris. She had been to the Anglesey Militia's cricket match and found it dull."

Sunday, May 31st:

"Ordination Sunday."

Monday, June 1st:

"Mary Sackville-West to luncheon, she and Hugh and Mollie rode afterwards, Hugh as far as Llanfair when he had to turn back. The rest of the ride was over new country and great fun. Emmie and Vincent Johnson [*the two youngest children, then aged 15 and 13, of Grace Vincent's brother, the Rev. Canon William Johnson*] arrived, bad account of Edward's eyes, he is being treated in a hospital in Dublin." [*Their brother Edward was then aged 20.*]

Tuesday, June 2nd:

"Very fine day, Norris Wyatt and his sister called."

Wednesday, June 3rd:

"Eva and Mollie went to the Sackville-Wests for tennis, rather a good party — play good and day fine."

Thursday, June 4th:

"Marked the tennis ground [*at Treborth Uchaf*], and played for the first time this season. Sent for new net. Did not go to the Militia sports." [*The Royal Anglesey Engineer Militia for whose "athletic sports" an invitation had been received.*]

Friday, June 5th:

"Rain came, which was much wanted and did not stop until 5 o'clock, when Mother and Mollie planted things. Hugh went to Bangor in the dogcart to a meeting about the dog show."

Saturday, June 6th:

"Will went to dinner with Mr and Mrs Gurney at 8 o'clock in the evening."

Thursday, June 11th:

[*An invitation to 'Mrs Vincent and Party' had been received for this day from Lieutenant-Colonel Hampton-Lewis of Henllys Hall, Beaumaris and Officers of the Royal Anglesey Engineers to an 'At Home' with dancing at the Bulkeley Arms Hotel in Beaumaris.*]

Tuesday, June 16th:

[*Members of the family attended a 'Grand Concert' at the Bangor Skating Rink — which largely comprised Mendelssohn's 'Hymn of Praise'. The orchestra included their friend Lionel Sackville-West as one of the eight violins.*]

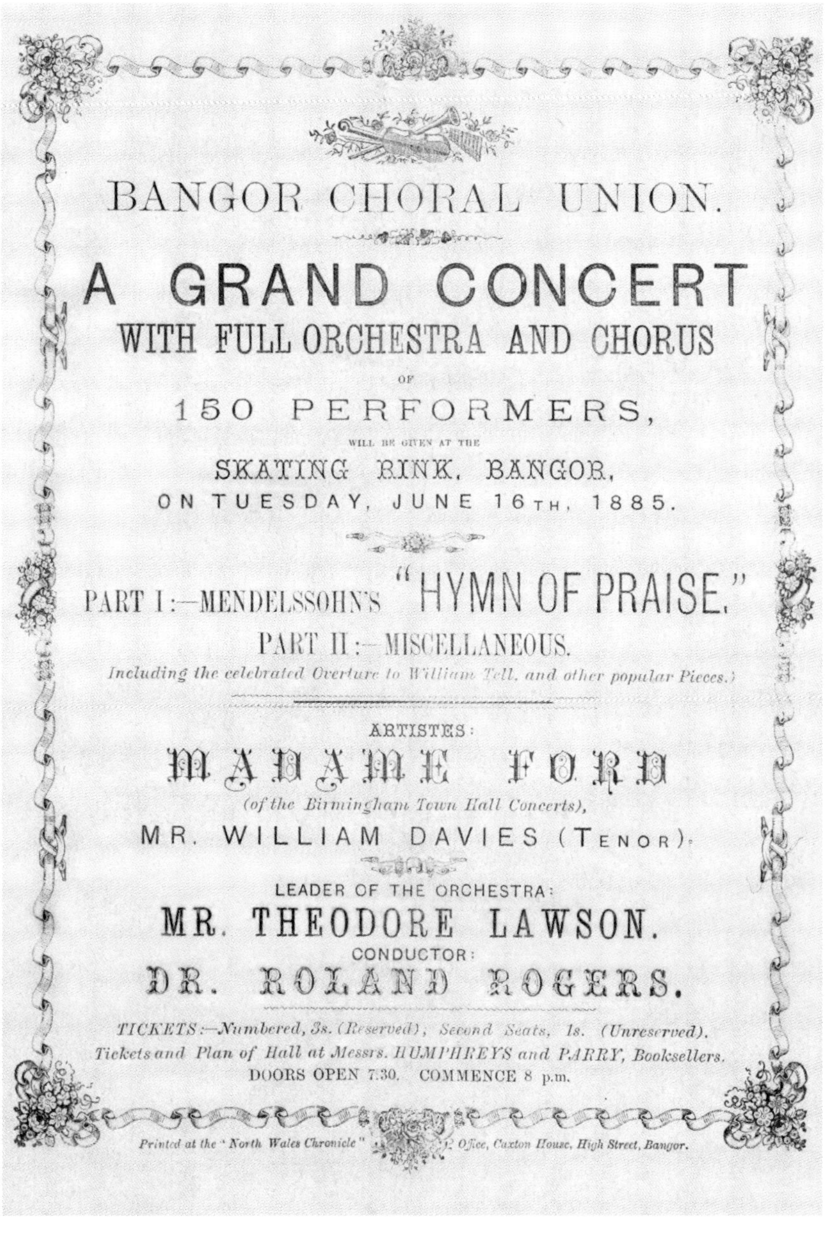

Thursday, June 25th:

"Mother, Georgie and Mollie drove to Llanfairpwll to the organ opening [*at St Mary's Church, at 3 p.m., given by Dr Roland Rogers who was at the time the organist of Bangor Cathedral*]. Afterwards went to an "At Home" [*held by the Rev. and Mrs Edwards at the Llanfairpwll rectory*]. A great many people there. The boys — Hugh, Will, Gustie, Mr Kindersley, Mr Wait and Lionel Sackville-West went to Carnarvon to play the tennis club there, and beat them easily. Mr Wait lunched here."

Friday, June 26th:

[*Gus had received an invitation to dinner in the University College Hall from the Principal, H.R. Reichel.*]

"Gus went to this dinner, which was rather dull. Mr Wood, [*from Colwyn Bay, a fellow student and*] a friend of Gustie came in the afternoon to tennis. Ffrangcon Davies [*the curate of Conwy*] was here and sung some new songs very well. Very hot day."

Monday, June 29th:

"[*Mollie*] spent the day in making a dress for Georgie."

Tuesday, June 30th:

"Georgie went to Llanrhyddlad and Dora Watkin-Davies came here."

Wednesday, July 1st:

"Gustie and Mollie went out with the Sackville-Wests in the *Miramar* and sailed around Anglesea. Mollie stayed that night at Lime Grove." [*The* Miramar *was a steam launch belonging to Colonel George McCorquodale, of Gadlys, Llansadwrn, near Menai Bridge.*]

Thursday, July 2nd:

"Mollie brought Cecilie Sackville-West home to luncheon. Mother and Will went to Penmaenmawr to play at the tennis club and to call on some people there. Had a very pleasant afternoon at home. Everyone nice and the weather good, heavy mist came on in the evening so that the trains could not be seen passing [*on the Bangor to Caernarfon line, which passed through the Vincents' land*]."

Friday, July 3rd:

"Eleanor Edwards spent the day here. Mrs Will [*wife of their cousin Will Wynne Jones*] came over from Carnarvon and brought Margaret [*their daughter*] and a Miss Cornish with her. The Rathbones called. Lil went to Bangor with Emmie Johnson. Same mist came on as had come on the night before. Babs not well, her arm bad."

Saturday, July 4th:

"Emmie and Vincent Johnson went home today [*after staying at Treborth Uchaf for a month*]. Will played cricket, Gustie watched cricket, Hugh went to the office. Lil and Dora went to Menai Bridge. Mollie enjoyed life because there were no visitors. No letter from Babs. Eva better, Georgie all right."

Sunday, July 5th:

"Went to the Cathedral in the morning. Mr Kindersley and Mr Wait arrived in the evening and stayed to supper. Went down to the covert after supper with the dogs."

Wednesday, July 8th:

"Rather wet day. Two youngest Hugheses and their governess to play tennis in the afternoon. Wet afternoon. Governess — Swiss — sings well."

Saturday, July 11th:

"Hugh went to Dublin, thence to Killarney. Will played cricket."

Sunday, July 12th:

"Will Wynne-Jones preached in the Cathedral. Mollie lunched at Canonry and spent the night there. Will and Gus rowed Will back [*the 7 miles to Caernarfon*]."

Monday, July 13th:

"Wet day, Eva and Georgie went into Bangor. Mollie stayed still at Canonry."

Tuesday, July 14th:

[*A telegram arrived from Ted Vincent reading: 'Will is seventeenth on the Indian Civil List. We are awfully glad. Marks one seven one seven.' This was a great achievement, the ICS being a most prestigious and highly competed-for career.*]

"Heard Will's place on the Indian Civil List, all much delighted. H. Mandel Jones came to stay. Will and Mollie went to Carnarvon to look at a tridarn for Lil, were most unsuccessful and both very tired, having walked many miles during their search." [*A tridarn is a uniquely Welsh type of 3-tier dresser comprising an upper, undivided display level; a middle pair of cupboards, slightly recessed; and a lower drawer and cupboard unit. The tridarn became the centre-piece of many North Wales farmhouse living rooms from 1650 onwards.*]

Wednesday, July 15th, St Swithin's:

"A good deal of wet. Played tennis. Went in the afternoon to call on Mrs Symes and Mrs Douglas. Went on to Bangor, did some shopping, not a high class day. Will played cricket." [*Mrs Symes lived at a fine Georgian house named Gorphwysfa, which had been built close to the mainland end of the Menai Suspension Bridge by the family of the earls of Lucan, for use when travelling to their estates in Ireland. The house is today known as Y Glyn.*]

Thursday, July 16th:

"Ted came down from Dolgelly at 6 o'clock. Lil, church. Tennis. Music. Will played tennis at Carnarvon."

Friday, July 17th:

"Wettish day. In the evening Mollie played tennis. Gus and H. Mandel Jones and Georgie and Lil bathed. Will had day [*in the mountains of Snowdonia*] at Ogwen."

[*Probably in celebration of William's examination success, he and Mollie went to London in the second half of July. They visited family friends and made theatre visits, for which several programmes are preserved with the diary. On Wednesday, July 22nd Will and Mollie attended a performance of* Olivia—*a play in four acts by W.G. Wills, based on an episode in* The Vicar of Wakefield—*at Henry Irving's Royal Lyceum with Ellen Terry in the title role and Irving himself as the Vicar of Wakefield. Henry Irving (1838-1905) had engaged Ellen Terry (1847-1928) as his leading lady in 1878. Their partnership lasted for 24 years and dominated the English stage. He became the first actor-knight in 1895 and she was made a Dame in 1925. The portrayal of Squire Thornhill in this production of* Olivia *transformed William Terriss from struggling actor to one of the most popular actors of his day. In 1897 he was assassinated by a lunatic as he entered the Adelphi theatre.*]

Mollie recorded her impressions of the production:

"Ellen Terry was more charming than the first time I'd seen her and Irving was better as the Vicar than as Benedict. Terris acted wonderfully. I have never heard such a lovely voice as Ellen Terry's. Ellen Terry's first dress was first a quilted petticoat with a looped up over-skirt of chintz and a cap, light hair, shoes with square toes and buckles. Her second dress was crimson brocaded silk with a long train and with a long black cloak, lined and trimmed with fur, which she threw on to return home with her father. The ringing of the village bells and the old spinet when they are singing the quartet are some of the parts that strike one most. Very hot but worth a great deal of trouble to see Ellen Terry, Henry Irving, W. Terriss."

Henry Irving and Ellen Terry in a publicity photograph for the 1885 production of *Olivia.*

Thursday, July 23rd:

"Will and Mollie went to lunch at the Harrisons', 14 Dawson Place, and went afterwards to the Grosvenor with Mary Harrison and had coffee afterwards at a jolly French place."

[With their brother Ted and his wife Babs, Will and Mollie also attended an evening concert given by the Strauss Orchestra conducted by Eduard Strauss, with music by Donizetti, Johann Strauss, Liszt and Eduard Strauss.]

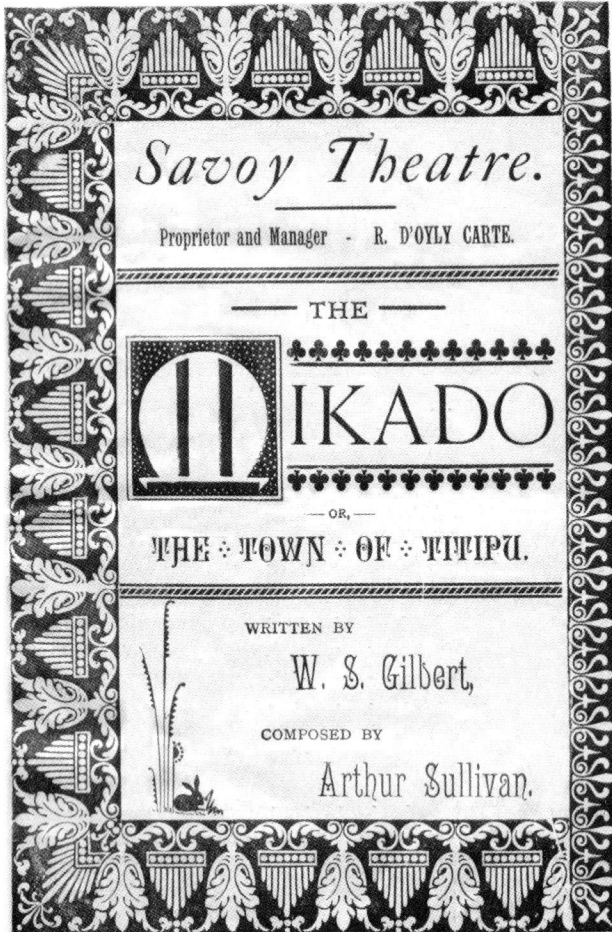

Savoy Theatre.

Proprietor and Manager - R. D'OYLY CARTE.

THE

MIKADO

— OR, —

THE ⬩ TOWN ⬩ OF ⬩ TITIPU.

WRITTEN BY

W. S. Gilbert,

COMPOSED BY

Arthur Sullivan.

Friday, July 24th:

"Mollie and Will saw *The Mikado* [*at D'Oyly Carte's Savoy Theatre*].

Saturday, July 25th:

"Mollie spent this afternoon with Edmund and Babs in London. Went to Covent Garden for the first time, ordered Lil's orange blossom [*for her marriage to Jack Lloyd-Williams which was to take place on August 11th*]. Went to tea [*at Selim Selim Freres, 92 Piccadilly, a fashionable Oriental Tea Room and Flower Bazaar*], very jolly and pretty. Day frightfully hot. Mollie was sent off alone to the Harrisons'."

Sunday, July 26th:

"Mr Shipley to dinner at Fulham [*at the home of their brother Ted*]. Mary and S. Harrison came down in the afternoon to fetch Will and Mollie to walk in the park with them."

Monday, July 27th: [*This entry is written by Ted Vincent*]

"MAV [*Babs*] and MMV [*Mollie*] went to luncheon at 34 Elm Park Gardens, South Kensington with Mrs Arthur Leach [*sister of Babs Vincent*]. Then shopped and came to tea at 1 Brick Court [*Ted's chambers*], Temple with Llewelyn Wynne-Jones [*the Vincents' second cousin*], Ford Williams and JEV. Then to dinner at C.L. Shipley's, Dulwich College. Dinner followed by school concert. *Dulce Domum* sung very badly. Home to 4 Fulham Palace Road at 12.45 – key forgotten – little Mary came to the door in Ulster and nightshirt.

Friday, July 31st:

[*The family are now back at Treborth preparing for Lil's wedding.*]

"Will came back from Brecon —'B' was very kind and Will enjoyed himself very much. D.W.E. Thomas asked to come to Treborth sometime in August. The Old Boys' match was rather a failure. Little Wait [*the teacher*] came to say adieu. Eva in one of her brightest moods."

Saturday, August 1st:

"Large number of ducks died. Jack [*the bridegroom*] arrived. Uncle W. staying here." [*The Rev. William Johnson, brother of Grace Vincent.*]

Monday, August 3rd:

"Will, Hugh and Uncle William went shooting at Cerig Llewelen [*Llewelyn*] —7 ducks, 6 snipe, 2 plover, 2 waterhen. The hotel very troublesome. Morgan thinks of prosecuting them. [*Mollie*] went to see Miss Barber."

Monday, August 10th:

[*Ted and Babs arrived from London.*]

Tuesday, August 11th, Lil's wedding day:

[*Ellen Augusta Crawley Vincent was married at Christ Church Caernarfon to John Jordan Lloyd-Williams, M.A. Oxon, lecturer in Classics at St David's College, Lampeter, and tutor-in-charge of Lampeter College School. The wedding was conducted by the Vincent cousin and current vicar of Caernarfon, the Rev. Will Wynne-Jones assisted by the father of the bridegroom, the Rev. Evan Williams, vicar of Nantcwnlle, Cardiganshire.*]

"For two or three days the weather had been stormy and wet, and the night before the 11th the wind had been worse than ever, no one slept much and at 5 we were all awake, looking at the weather, it was very bad, the rain coming down in sheets. At 7 o'clock the Davies carriage came to fetch us. We left Lil ready dressed, and met the carriage coming for her. We arrived at Carnarvon at 8.20, found Will Wynne-Jones ready, then came Jack with Hugh. The boys had driven over in the dogcart earlier. The service was all nice and nobody cried, not because they weren't sorry. Jack and Lil drove home together, 4 in the dogcart, the rest in the Davies carriage, all very ready for breakfast at 12. The Davies girls came over, had some cake and we all walked down the park to the station to see Lil and Jack off to Treiorwerth [*Bodedern, Anglesey*], the day then finer. Came back after they were gone, had dinner at 3, saw the Williamses off. Went to Treborth Hall, had tea, played billiards, danced in the hall, came home, went to bed. Water lilies, wedding presents, weariness of mind and body strongest memories left."

John Jordan Lloyd-Williams, who married Lil Vincent on August 11th 1885.

Wednesday, August 12th:

"Ted and Babs went to Dolgelly to spend the first anniversary of their wedding day. Came back on the 13th, had been to see the Vaughans at Nannau."

Thursday, August 13th:

[*There was a sale of work at the Masonic Hall in aid of the Bangor Diocesan Branch of the Ladies Home Mission Association and the Additional Curates Society. Mollie Vincent was one of the stallholders and £21 was raised.*]

Friday, August 14th:

"Mollie went to Penmon with the Cathedral choirboys' treat. Lovely day."

[*The following report in the* North Wales Chronicle *is preserved in the diary.*]

"The excursion of the boys of the cathedral choir which the kindness of Miss Wynne-Jones and Miss Sackville-West, liberally assisted by many friends interested in the happiness and welfare of the boys has now made annual, took place this year at Penmon with the usual good fortune. The day chosen, Friday last, August 14th, proved exceptionally fine and the party were made independent of wind or tide by the steam launch *Miramar,* most generously lent for the occasion by her owner, Colonel McCorquodale. The landing which took some time, was no sooner effected, than an exciting cricket match, Decani v. Cantoris [*the two sides of the choir*] was commenced. It was reluctantly interrupted for dinner and resumed immediately afterwards. This resulted in a success for Cantoris. The same sides were then strengthened by outsiders and the match was played again with the same result. The umpiring of the assistant organist and the batting of one of the minor canons excited admiration. The wishing well at the Priory and the Penmon lighthouse were visited. Then followed tea upon the grass, a meal much appreciated by folk whose appetites, sea-air and cricket had sharpened. The way home was enlivened by song, but all too soon for the merry voyagers, Garth Point was reached, 'Auld Lang Syne' sang and parting cheers for kind hosts given. Thus ended a most successful day."

The cricketing boy choristers of Bangor Cathedral. Bertie Sackville-West is seated second from left. (University of Wales, Bangor)

Friday, August 21st:

[*Will's friend from his Brecon days, Richard Budworth, arrived on a visit.*]

Saturday, August 22nd:

"Went to an 'At Home' at the Rathbones' Crowds of people there. Mother, Eva, Babs and Mollie went there; Edmund, Gus and Hugh at Carnarvon playing tennis. Will and Mr Budworth at cricket at Bangor. Georgie had Trixie and Olga Gilbert Smith to tea."

Sunday, August 23rd:

"Lil and Jack went to Ireland yesterday, are at the Gresham Hotel today. Went with the Davieses to Llanddwyn in the *Pioneer*. Started at 10 o'clock, Mother, Mollie, Hugh, Georgie, Edmund. Gustie, Eva, Babs and Will stayed at home. Rather a grey morning when we started, got there safely, picked up shells, had a large luncheon. Mary Davies sketched, Edie [*Edith Davies*] and Mollie V. and the boys went out in a boat to shoot curlews, never got within a hundred yards of them. Water very green, rocks very black, birds very wary, sportsmen not keen. Then the boat people landed and some of us looked at the lifeboat, which has not been used since 1877, after which we all bathed, the girls in one bay, the boys in another, after which we all built sandcastles and Arthur fell into the water. Then tea, then a walk, then we all wished at the wishing well which is covered by half an old boat. Then we were all rather sorry to get back into the boat to come home. However, we sang songs all the way home. Carnarvon Castle looked very jolly as we passed, Hugh had a shot at some herons on our way up, and Claude Gilbert Smith sang songs to the moon. We landed under the Tube [*Britannia Tubular Bridge*] at half past eight and were met by Will, Mr Budworth and the dogs."

Wednesday, September 2nd:

"Lil and Jack went away after being here from August 28th. Mr King was here for a few days as usual, very nice, he went away on Sunday night the 30th."

Wednesday, September 9th:

"Edmund and Babs went away after being here since August 10th. Mary Cotterill at Carnarvon [*vicarage*]. The archdeacon [*father of both Will Wynne-Jones and Mary Cotterill*] has not been very well but is better again. Weather has begun to get cold but still jolly and bright."

Friday, September 18th:

[*An invitation was received for this day, from Mrs Hugh Hughes of Garth View House for an 'At Home' with music.*]

"Hugh and Mollie went to this, it was rather fun. Drove back with Edith and Mary Davies."

Monday, September 21st:

"Will at Llaniestyn shooting [*staying with his Johnson relatives at the rectory*]. Mr Budworth went away on September 17th. Mary Cotterill and Jessie Wynne-Jones and their children here to spend the day on September 16th. Hugh out shooting with Captain Morgan. Shot 24 brace of partridge. [*Captain Francis Mansel Morgan of Plas Coed Mor, Llanfairpwll.*] Eva lunched at Carnarvon with the Wynne-Joneses. Mother, Georgie and Mollie went to a 'Ladies' Home Mission' at the Cathedral. Mollie called on Mrs Reichel. Dora Ramsay came to luncheon and went to the meeting. Heard that the Bishop of Edinburgh [*Mary Cotterill's father-in-law*] had not long to live, about 6 months (Sir James Paget says). The Wynne-Joneses and Cotterills greatly troubled about it. Llewie Wynne-Jones and Maude Scovell coming tomorrow for 2 days. [*The Scovells were family friends in Ireland.*] The family all well, away and at home. Weather still fine especially today."

Thursday, September 24th:

"Norah's puppies born."

Saturday, September 26th:

"Snow on the mountains and the weather very cold. Mollie and Gus went to the Wyatts' to tennis, drove home in a storm of hail and rain. Mollie had come from Parkgate that day. Mollie had a new dress from Madame Knight. Loo Wynne-Jones had been here for 5 days. Went from here to Carnarvon. Will still at Llaniestyn."

Sunday, September 27th:

"The archdeacon was at the morning service, Will Wynne-Jones preached. Owen Evans [*Minor Canon at Bangor Cathedral*] gone to Lampeter."

Monday, September 28th:

"Hugh and Gus in Anglesey with Norris Wyatt. Milly Owen came to say goodbye before her wedding which is on the 6th of next month."

Tuesday, September 29th, St Michael and All Angels:

"The boys, Hugh and Gus still in Anglesey with Norris Wyatt, to come back this evening. A goose for dinner, one sent to Babs and Ted. Eva and Mollie went to Bangor to tea at Lime Grove. Went to see Meg on their way back and found her alone [*at the archdeaconry, her parents probably being at Treiorwerth in Anglesey*], so Mollie stayed with her that night. Boys had shot in Anglesey 14 partridges, 1 hare (shot by Gus—his first), 1 snipe, (4 pheasants — over which cast a veil). Bishop Reichel [*brother of Principal Reichel of the Bangor College*] installed Bishop of Meath."

Wednesday, September 30th:

"Meg went to Treiorwerth. Mollie came home. Sent partridges to Babs. Mother has a bad cold. The day terribly wet and windy. Will back from Llaniestyn. Mollie heard from Babs this morning."

Thursday, October 1st:

"Gus and Mollie went out with the Barbers in the *Tysilio*. It was rather a rough day so they only sailed between the ferry and Penmon all day. They went outside Penmon twice but only a little way just to see how rough it was. On board were Alice Greg Hughes [*née Barber*], Tom, Alfred and Frank Barber, Lionel and Cecilie Sackville-West, and four other people. After they came in, Gus and Mollie spent the evening at Lime Grove."

Friday, October 2nd:

"Eva drove to Treiorwerth with Will Wynne-Jones so that Joe Cotterill [*his brother-in-law*] should see her, and tell what was to be done for her. It was a terribly wet and windy day. Mr Kirkpatrick arrived at 5 o'clock to spend the evening on his way to Ireland. Mollie went to dine at Treborth Hall instead of Mother who had been asked but was not well enough to go. She met there Professor Michael Foster and Mr Reichel, the evening was rather dull. Gus entered himself at the college for the year. A great many new students are entered."

Saturday, October 3rd:

"Will, Gus and Mollie went to the college to hear Professor Michael Foster deliver an address, and open the new Biological School. Mr Darwin, son of the Darwin was there, a small man with a light beard and grey eyes, a quiet sort of face. Professor Michael Foster was of the mild-eyed, melancholy 'lotus-eater' type. There was a great crowd at the Lecture, Gus thought about five hundred. Old Mr Davies surpassed himself as chairman, forgetting Mr Foster's name though he had stayed at Treborth Hall since yesterday. [*Richard Davies of Treborth Hall was at this time the Lord Lieutenant of Anglesey and Vice-President of the University College in Bangor.*] Eva came back from Treiorwerth. Joe Cotterill says she wants iron, and that she wants care. Heard from Ted this morning. Eva and George buried four bottles of nuts, the grave being like Moses', except to them. The Marquis' first day with the hounds today but none of the boys went."

Sunday, October 4th:

"Went to Cathedral this morning, weather fine but cold in the morning, very wet and windy in the evening. Georgie and Mollie went to the 'Tin' and got very wet."

Monday, October 5th:

"Harvest Home at the 'Tin', rather a wet horrid day."

Tuesday, October 6th:

"The day the boys had chosen to shoot over the place, Norris Wyatt came earlier and it rained all day without stopping, and they were wet through twice. They shot all day in spite of the rain and shot nineteen head of game, mostly rabbits."

Wednesday, October 7th:

"Ted came down from London on *Times* business."

Thursday, October 8th:

"Rained all day, it was rather a tiresome day altogether. Will went to Dublin at 12.50 We were all very tired and glad to go to bed."

[*William Vincent was beginning a two year course of training for the Indian Civil Service at Trinity College, Dublin. This could have been done at other universities, including Oxford and Cambridge. His choice of university may have been influenced not only by the proximity of Dublin to North Wales, but also by the fact that his best school friend, Harry Griffith, was there studying medicine. Their fathers had been contemporaries at Oxford and the boys had been together at both Friars' School, Bangor, and Christ College, Brecon. Both were keen cricketers who played in the school XI and subsequently for the Old Breconians. Harry's home was the vicarage in Pentraeth, Anglesey, and so they were able to spend time together in term and during holidays.*]

Friday, October 9th:

"Fine day, boys shot a few pheasants."

[*On this day Hugh Vincent at the office of Charles Jones, Solicitors, Caernarfon, received one of the first sixpenny telegrams from his brother Edmund Vincent informing the family of his arrival by train at 4 a.m. the following morning.*]

[*The entries from October 13th to October 19th are made by Grace Vincent (GV).*]

Tuesday, October 13th:

"The Sackville-Wests came to get an hour with GV bringing a peacock. LW [Lionel Sackville-West] went to Conway to see Ffrangcon Davies who had had an accident, found him better. Mollie and Georgie went to Lampeter in company with Mr and Mrs Bankes-Price."

[*Mrs Bankes-Price and her brother Reverend Rowland Williams, the vice-principal of St David's College, Lampeter, were cousins of Grace Vincent. The Rev. David Bankes-Price, vicar of Llangelynin, near Conwy, was a former student of St David's. He had been curate to Grace's father, the elder William Johnson, at Llanfaethlu from 1857 to 1863. His two sons, William and Sidney, had been among those Friars' School pupils who, along with Will Vincent, had followed the headmaster, Daniel Lewis Lloyd, to Christ College, Brecon. Sidney was an exact contemporary of Will's and his presence in London as a medical student at the Middlesex hospital may well have provided Will with a friend from home whilst he was engaged in the London part of his preparation for the Indian Civil Service entrance examinations.*]

Wednesday, October 14th:

"Mr Fairchild came over to shoot with Hugh, or rather to see Hugh shoot. Would not have luncheon but had some tea."

Thursday, October 15th:

"Potatoes began to be lifted up and sold. Great event at Lampeter which passed off very successfully." [*The 'Great event at Lampeter' referred to above, was a visit by the Archbishop of Canterbury and the laying of the foundation stone of a new building at St David's College. In attendance were all the Welsh bishops and a large body of the clergy.*]

Saturday, October 17th:

"Eva went to the Sackville-Wests, Gustie to football. Eva ever much more poorly."

Sunday, October 18th:

"GV and Eva drove to Bangor. Canon Williams preached strong political sermon against disestablishment. Mr Arnold left the church in the middle."

Monday, October 19th:

"Mr Roberts of Bryn Adda [*a prominent Bangor solicitor*] came to look at filly for a friend. HV [*Hugh Vincent*] rode her after luncheon."

[*On her return to Treborth Uchaf, Mollie Vincent added this retrospective account of her visit to Lampeter.*]

Tuesday, October 13th:

"Mollie and Georgie got to Lampeter safely and were met there by Lil and Jack who took them to their house. They first went into the drawing room which is very pretty and had wine and biscuits, then into the other room and had some tea and chicken, then went out and saw the boys playing football. Next morning, the 14th, went down and saw the college. Went into the hall, library and chapel. Saw all the men parading for the next day's procession in the quad. The day was rather damp, saw all the professors, saw the marquee which was very large. Saw all the food ready cooked in the kitchens and never saw so much together. Uncle William [*Rev. Canon William Johnson*] came that afternoon, also [*his cousin*] Mr H. Wynne-Jones. He told us that Llewie had decided to enter the church. Uncle William and Mr H. Wynne-Jones dined in hall that night." [*Mr H. Wynne-Jones was the Rev. Henry Wynne-Jones, brother to Archdeacon Wynne-Jones of Bangor. 'Llewie' was his son Llewelyn.*]

Thursday, October 15th:

"Were all up in pretty good time, then went down to the college, the day not very bad but not good. Then we went down to the station where we saw Colonel Sackville-West. Talked with him for a little and then went and sat in one of the hostels until the train which was to bring the Archbishop came. We saw our Bishop and the Bishop of St David's and the Bishop of Llandaff, and many hundreds of very plain parsons. Then we walked to the college and got on a platform near the foundation stone and waited for the procession to come, which at last happened, though the bishops had taken a long time to dress in their coronation robes. The Archbishop's train was held up by two boys from Jack's school, Basil Jayne and a boy called Georgie Roberts. The crozier was carried by Mr Alfred Edwards, the late Dean's brother. The pastoral staff of St David's was carried by someone, there was also a staff with a silver mitre, though I do not know to which bishop it belonged. The service was read partly by the Bishop of St David's and the address by the Archbishop. The Archbishop was the youngest looking of the bishops with brown hair combed straight back from his forehead like the late Dean's [*Dean Edwards of Bangor*]. He had a very splendid face and voice, and could be heard very distinctly by almost everyone though the crowd was so great that when the Creed was said the ending clause could be heard five times echoing away. The hymns were kept together by a band which sounded very well. After the laying of the stone was over, everyone went to the tent which was laid with luncheon for 1,000 people. After the eating was over, the speeches began. The Archbishop spoke first and much the best. Then the Bishop of St David's, pretty good; Lord Emlyn very well; our Bishop like a sermon and no one pretended to listen; Dean Vaughan very gently; Mr Cecil Raikes, Mr Talbot, Colonel Sackville-West and some more people who weren't heard. There seemed very few ladies. Lady Lisbon [*Lisburne?*] sat on the Archbishop's right hand. She looked very young, was a good deal got up, large dark eyes and light hair which was worn on top of her head. She had a very tight bodice made of a sort of brown and gold tissue in a large pattern. I did not look at the skirt. There was also in the tent having luncheon one old woman or lady in full Welsh costume, with a high hat."

ST. DAVID'S COLLEGE, LAMPETER,

Visit of the Archbishop of Canterbury,

October 15th, 1885.

ADMISSION TO THE CEREMONY AND THE LUNCHEON.

THIS CARD MUST BE BROUGHT AND PRESENTED ON APPLICATION.

Tuesday, November 3rd:

"Hamilton Poole came here [*from Caernarfon*] to stay for the balls.[*These were the hunt balls at Beaumaris.*] Ellen Johnson [*daughter of Canon Johnson*] had come the day before. By mistake the dresses didn't come in time so Georgie was not able to go at all the first night so Mollie and Ellen Johnson went. It was a very good ball and the Lady Patroness quite the best looking one there had been for years and Bob Wynne-Jones made a very good and pleasant-looking comptroller and [*his sister*] Meg looked after everyone and was very nice. Bob had brought as his party Mr and Mrs George Younger [*of the Edinburgh and Alloa brewing family*], Dr Pringle, Mr Yale, Mr McKenzie, Miss McKenzie, Jin Marshall. The Ramsays went with us and looked very well, Dora and Violet, Dora in yellow, Violet white. There were plenty of men and the ball was a great success."

Wednesday, November 4th:

"Will and Hamilton Poole went to the steeplechase. Mollie and Hugh were to have gone to the dinner, but the evening turned out very wet so they didn't go."

Thursday, November 5th:

"Waited all day for our dresses which 'never came'. Will at last went up to Chester to look for them, finally after all hope was given up, they appeared at half past seven. Eva had gone to the Ramsays', so the boys drove to Beaumaris and took her frock with them and we followed and got there about half past ten. It was a very crowded ball, with double the number of boys to men but it went off very well. Almost everybody was dressed in black or white, mostly white and no flowers, except the lady Patroness' bouquet which was very huge and sweet given her by Bob Wynne. The best looking girls in the room were the Lady Patroness [*Miss Pennant Lloyd*], the Hon. Mrs Stanhope, Miss Alice Douglas Pennant and Miss Hilda Douglas Pennant. The best dancers were the Miss Turners. It was Georgie's first ball and we all thought she looked nicest. The Ramsays had very nice dresses and were very much admired. The Lady Patroness did not ride at the head of the procession."

[*The following newspaper report of the above event is preserved in the diary.*]

THE ANGLESEY HUNT

"Thursday week, was, in all respects, one of the most joyous days of the year in Beaumaris. The greatest happiness prevailed. The weather was fine; the attendance at the time-honoured procession was the largest that has been remembered, and all passed off with the greatest *éclat*. In our hearing at Beaumaris in former happy days, one of the heartiest Englishmen now alive — nobleman we should say—the Right Hon. Baron Bramwell, when presiding in the Beaumaris Assize Court said: He was much delighted with his tour which had closed in the most delightful locality, he believed, in all Her Majesty's dominions. Assuredly had that lover par excellence of fine old English pastime been present on the occasion under notice, he would have been heartily pleased with the exceedingly pleasant termination of the Anglesey Hunt week. The 'Fifth of November' used to be in grammar school a red-letter day; and certainly, Beaumaris had much reason to be proud of the procession which passed and returned through its avenues upon the closing day of the Anglesey Hunt week. The huntsman and his fine pack of harriers led the procession, followed by many of the nobility and gentry of the sister counties of Anglesey and Carnarvon on horseback and in carriages, all evidently delighted with the week's enjoyment. 'Rosy health' was everywhere apparent; the very greatest credit was given to the secretary and assistant secretary, both of whom were indefatigable throughout the entire week's proceedings. At the meetings, and likewise at the balls, held at the Bulkeley Arms Hotel, Beaumaris, there were, indeed, most excellent assemblies of the nobility and gentry of the sister counties of Anglesey and Carnarvon.

At 'The Ladies' Ordinary', the comptroller (Sir R.W. Bulkeley Bart.) proposed the toast of 'Her most Gracious Majesty the Queen, the Prince and Princess of

Wales and the other members of the Royal Family' together with 'the Lord-lieutenants and other magistrates of the sister counties', for whom that very popular gentleman, Captain Pritchard-Rayner, by unanimous request, responded. Captain Lovatt returned cordial thanks for the toast of 'The Army', and Captain Rawnsley, R.N. for 'The Navy'. The comptroller proposed 'the Bishop and Clergy of the Diocese,' for whom the Rev. J.L. Kyffin and Rev. J.Wynne-Jones happily responded. After which the comptroller, in appropriate terms proposed the toast of the evening 'The Lady Patroness,' for whom her father, Mr Pennant Lloyd responded and a most enjoyable evening was spent.

The hotel and town hall were decorated by Miss Williams with flags etc. kindly lent by Sir Richard Williams-Bulkeley, deputy comptroller.

Among the company present during the week were:- Sir R.H. Williams-Bulkeley (deputy comptroller), Colonel and Mrs Hampton-Lewis, Major and Mrs Fletcher, Major and Mrs Lloyd, Tregaian; Mr and Mrs Massey, and Misses Massey, Cornelyn; Mr and Mrs U.B. Corbett, Captain C.G. Duff, the Hon. W.W. Vivian, the Hon. Claud Vivian, Captain J. Bulkeley Price, and the Misses Bulkeley Price, Mr and Mrs Pennant Lloyd, Miss Pennant Lloyd (Lady Patroness), the Hon. M. Eden, Mr P. Tatton Cork, Captain Lovatt, Mr Bax Ironside, Captain Pritchard-Rayner, Mr C.F. Priestley, Mr and Mrs O. Lloyd J. Evans, Broom Hall; Captain and Mrs Johnson, Mr, Mrs and Miss J.H. Gartside, Admiral Bythesea, Mr Henry Poole, Captain Stewart, Mr and Mrs Raple C. Williams, Mr, Mrs and Miss C. Edwards, Llanfair P.G.; Mr and Mrs T. Fanning Evans, the Rev. T. Lloyd and Mrs Kyffin, the Rev. and the Hon. Mrs Wynne-Jones, Miss Wynne-Jones, Mr G.W. Assheton-Smith, Mr and Mrs Williams, Trecastell; Mr H.R. Poole, Miss Risk, Miss Roberts, Mr T.W. Roberts, Dr R.E. Owen and Mrs Owen, Mr C. Heyworth, Captain Galbraith, Mr Fairbridge, Lady Ramsay and Misses Ramsay, Mrs Younger, Miss MacKenzie, Miss Hargreaves, Mrs White Griffith and Mrs Glynne Griffith, Mr W.A. de la B. Ramsay, Mr R.W. Peel, Mrs Hick, Mrs MacKenzie, Dr and Mrs Arthur Trevor, Mr and Mrs George E. Brooke, the Misses Vincent, Treborth; Mrs and Miss Griffith, Pentraeth Rectory; Mr E. P. Griffith, Mr H.R. Griffith, Mr and Mrs Rice Roberts, Mr Gwynedd Williams, Craigydon; Captain and Mrs Turner, Overhaul; Mr R. Bennett, Mr H. Tinsley, Mr Percy Luse, Mr T.W. Roberts, Mr D.H. Madeley, Mr N. Tindale Caril Worsley, Mr C.H. Tinsdale, Mr W.H. Vincent, Mr A.N. Wyatt, Mr C.E.H. Poole, Mr F. Hepworth, Mr J.E.J. Yale, Mr G. Younger, Mr J.J. Pringill, Mr A. Vincent, Mr W. Scott, Mr E.C. Kendall, Mr

F.G. Highgate, Mr E.V.D. Pierce, Mr W. G. Massey, Mr E. Massie, Mr E.M. Glegg, Mr H.A. Duff, Mr Kenworth MacKenzie, Captain W.M. Preston, Mr O.R. Williams, Mr R.K. Mainwaring, Mr C.E.J. Owen, Mr R. Dundas, Mr A.R. Peel, Mr and Mrs Collin Stanhope-Jones, Lady Penrhyn, the Misses Pennant, the Hon. Lincoln Stanhope, the Hon. Mrs Stanhope, Mrs Aspinall, Miss Heygate, Miss Williams, Mr and Mrs C. Morrall, Miss Lewis, the Deanery; Mr and Mrs Morgan Evans, Mrs Owen, Miss Tymonds, Mrs White Griffith, Miss Grant, Mr Arthur E. Wynne, Mr James G. Dobbie, Mr G.F. Pearson, Mr R. Carreg, Miss Carreg, Mr A.C. Stewart and Mr H.C. Vincent."

Tuesday, November 10th:

"Mother, Ellen Johnson, Hugh, Gustie and Mollie went to Beaumaris. Hugh and Mollie lunched at Trecastell, the rest at the Ramsays'. Drove over in the dogcart. Miss Barber had been here to hear all the Hunt news."

Wednesday, November 11th:

"Ellen Johnson, Hugh and Mollie went to a musical party at the Sackville-Wests'. Meg Wynne-Jones and Ella Ramsay were staying there. Everyone had very fine frocks and no one sang very well, but it went off very well."

Friday, November 13th:

[*There was 'A Grand Concert' this evening at Vaynol School, Penrhosgarnedd, Bangor, with proceeds in aid of the day and Sunday school funds. The first half of the programme was opened by a pianoforte solo given by Miss Mary Sackville-West; the second part commenced with a piano duet by the Misses Mary and Cecilie Sackville-West and also included the song 'On Wings Of Song' performed by Miss Mollie Vincent.*]

Sunday, December 13th:

"Elections over. Conservatives and Nationalists [*Irish Home Rule party*] together equal to Liberals. All Welsh members Liberal bar three. Conservatives in Wales gained votes since last election. [*This was the election that resulted in a hung Parliament and the brief continuation of Salisbury's minority Conservative administration which had come to power five months earlier on Gladstone's resignation. One local Liberal victory, however, was that of William Rathbone who, in the North Carnarvonshire constituency, polled 4562 votes for the Liberal party against the 2838 recorded by the Vincent family friend Henry Platt, the Conservative candidate.*]

"Eva at Treiorwerth. Ted coming down from London tonight. Hugh and he going over to Caer Ellen tomorrow about the poachers on the lake. Will in Dublin. Hugh and Gus working hard and playing football. Cathedral this morning and Penrhos this evening with Hugh and Gus to help in the choir."

Christmas Day, Friday, December 25th, 1885:

"Lil and Jack came down on Christmas Eve. Boiled toffees and sang hymns as usual, very 'misty moisty evening'. Christmas Day we all went to the Cathedral, came back and found our cards, had luncheon. Katie and Edie [*Davies*] came in and brought grapes, Penrhosgarnedd boys played football in the front field. Went to service at the 'Tin' at half past six, children sang carols. Came home, then dinner, then whisky and smoking, then bed. Heard from Babs and Ted, the rest of the family at home."

Saturday, December 26th:

"The Sackville-Wests to tea, Mr Shipley came at 7.30."

Monday, December 28th:

"All went to a dinner at Treborth Hall. Dance afterwards."

Tuesday, December 29th:

"Horrid day. Hugh, Will, Gus, Mollie, Eva, went to a dance at Trecastell which they all enjoyed tremendously. Got home at 4 a.m."

Wednesday, December 30th:

"Weather detestable."

Thursday, December 31st:

"New Year's Eve. Went to Lime Grove, all of us, great fun, snap-dragon games, general frivolity. Just home, now January 1st 1886, 12.20. Waiting for Hugh, Will and Gus who are walking. Mother and Mr Shipley talking politics. Lil in her wedding dress, tired and sleepy. General impression of the family that '85 has been a good year."

THE VINCENT FAMILY DIARY FOR 1886

Friday, January 1st 1886:

"<u>Present.</u> Mother, Mollie, Lil and Jack, Hugh, Eva, Will, Georgie, Gus, Mr Shipley.

Mollie and Hugh rode to Aber. Will went to a dance at Cemaes with Harry Griffith. [*Both were on vacation from Trinity College, Dublin*] Jessie Wynne-Jones to lunch. Violet and Allan Ramsay called to see Lil."

Saturday, January 2nd:

"Lionel Sackville-West and Will went to run; Will had a splendid day from Black Horse to Garth, running with Harry Griffith and came home through Bangor and found Lionel at Treborth."

[*For the months of January and February 1886, the family seems to have been so preoccupied socially that no one took responsibility for the diary entries. From notes and preserved invitations, the following events emerge:*

During the first week Will went to dances at Llanfaethlu and Llanfairynghornwy.

Mollie "had bad neuralgia for a fortnight".

'Mrs Vincent and Party' were invited to an 'At home' at Lime Grove on January 12th by invitation of Colonel W.E. Sackville-West and Miss Sackville-West. It was "very good value, all went except Mother".

For the 14th of January, 'Mr H.C. and Mr W.H. Vincent' were invited to a dance by Captain Kennedy and Officers of HMS Hotspur, held at the Ballroom, Soldiers' Point, Holyhead: "Hugh and Will enjoyed it very much".

Eva went to London on January 14th.

There is a preserved enrolment card in the name of Miss Grace Georgiana Vincent for lectures in German during the lent term of 1886.

Will went to Dublin January 18th

Hugh went to London January 20th.

During the month Mollie and Will went to Treiorwerth and Ted came home for a few days.

On February 19th Mollie and Mary Sackville-West went down to Lampeter and there are no more entries for that month. Mollie at least appears to have stayed with her sister Lil, now living in Lampeter, until the end of March.]

St David's Day, Monday, March 1ˢᵗ:

"Mother , Eva, Georgie, Gus at Treborth. Ted and Hugh in town [London].
Mollie and Lil at Lampeter. Will at TCD."

[Georgie and Gustie went to the St David's Day Dinner at the University
College of North Wales and Eva attended a St David's Day concert at the College.]

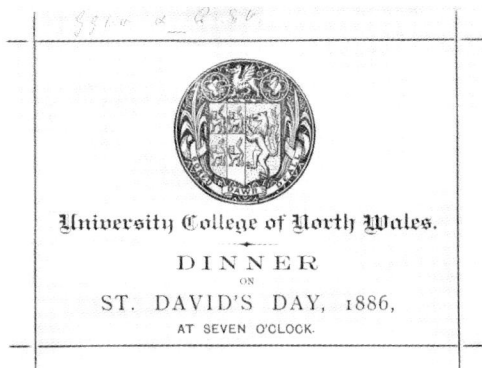

[On 4th March some members of the family attended a 'Grand Chamber
Concert' featuring visiting artistes at the Penrhyn Hall, Bangor. The evening
included music by Beethoven, Brahms, Chopin, Schubert and Liszt.]

"Mother went to Treiorwerth on March 6th and stayed until the 10th."

[For March 9th, Gus Vincent had received an invitation from Miss Pryce to
a party at the Canonry.] "Eva, Gus and Georgie went there and heard Mr Arnold
perform *The Death of Becket*. The result was unexpected, possibly ludicrous.
Music indifferent. Lots drawn for partners at supper, in which drawing Gustie
managed to have good luck."

"Will and HRG went to college dance [at *Trinity College, Dublin*], got up by
King, which was a great success. Will went to see Compton at the Gaiety, Dublin,
and also Miss Langtry in *The School for Scandal*." [Edward Compton and his
Compton Comedy Company toured the provinces from 1881 to 1918 with a classical
repertory. Lillie Langtry, 'the Jersey Lily', was born Emilie Charlotte Le Breton, and
was one of the first English society beauties to go on the stage. She had been an
intimate friend of the Prince of Wales (later Edward VII). Though never a great

actress, she was extremely popular and at the height of her fame at this period.]

"King came home with WHV on March 21st The latter [*Will*] went on to town [*London*] on the 23rd [*in part at least, in relation to his ICS training*].

Gus went to Lampeter on the 27th. Eva went to Treiorwerth on the same day.

King went back on the 29th on which day Mollie came back [*from Lampeter*]. Ted had a lot of work (Bryce v. Burden)."

"During this month the weather was terrible, more snow than has been known for many years and intense cold."

"Hugh and Will had a good time in London, saw Miss Langtry twice in *Lady of Lyons* and *Enemies* and saw *The Schoolmistress* at the Court."

[*Will gives a more detailed account of how he and Hugh saw the Boat Race on Saturday, 3rd April.*]

"We started at 1 o'clock and went down to Putney through great crowds. Hugh wanted to throw for coconuts but we had no time so he had to rest on his former glories. We dashed along the edge of the river, at times getting wet, until we got about 200 yards below the start. We saw the boats out and then watched carefully for the start. At the start Cambridge was ahead but Oxford pulled up and at Barnes were ahead. Between there and Mortlake, however, Pitman pulled his crew together and finally won by about a length. We went down as fast as we could to Hammersmith and then ran madly across to Mortlake to find that Cambridge had won though we had thought Oxford certain from having been ahead at Barnes. The crowd at the boat race was tremendous, lining the bank, rather rough and excited about the race, all wearing scraps of ribbon, very fairly good-natured as London crowds mostly seem to be. We came back rather down in the mouth to Putney and Will had to hurry off to a viva while Hugh went to work. Hugh is working very hard up in town. In the evening we went as aforesaid to the Court Theatre which we enjoyed immensely."

Monday, April 5th:

"Mother sold heffer for £5. 10. 0d. Will arrived at 2 in the morning to frighten Owen who was sleeping in the Upper [*a room above one of the ancient stone barns of the property*]. Owen appeared very much 'deshabillé' but ready for action, though somewhat relieved to find who the intruder was. Ramsays, Will Wynne-Jones, Lionel Sackville-West to luncheon on a cold day. Went to the covert and found a plover's nest."

Amateur-printed programme for a charity concert in Menai Bridge, attended by Mollie Vincent and her mother. Printing was a popular hobby at this time.

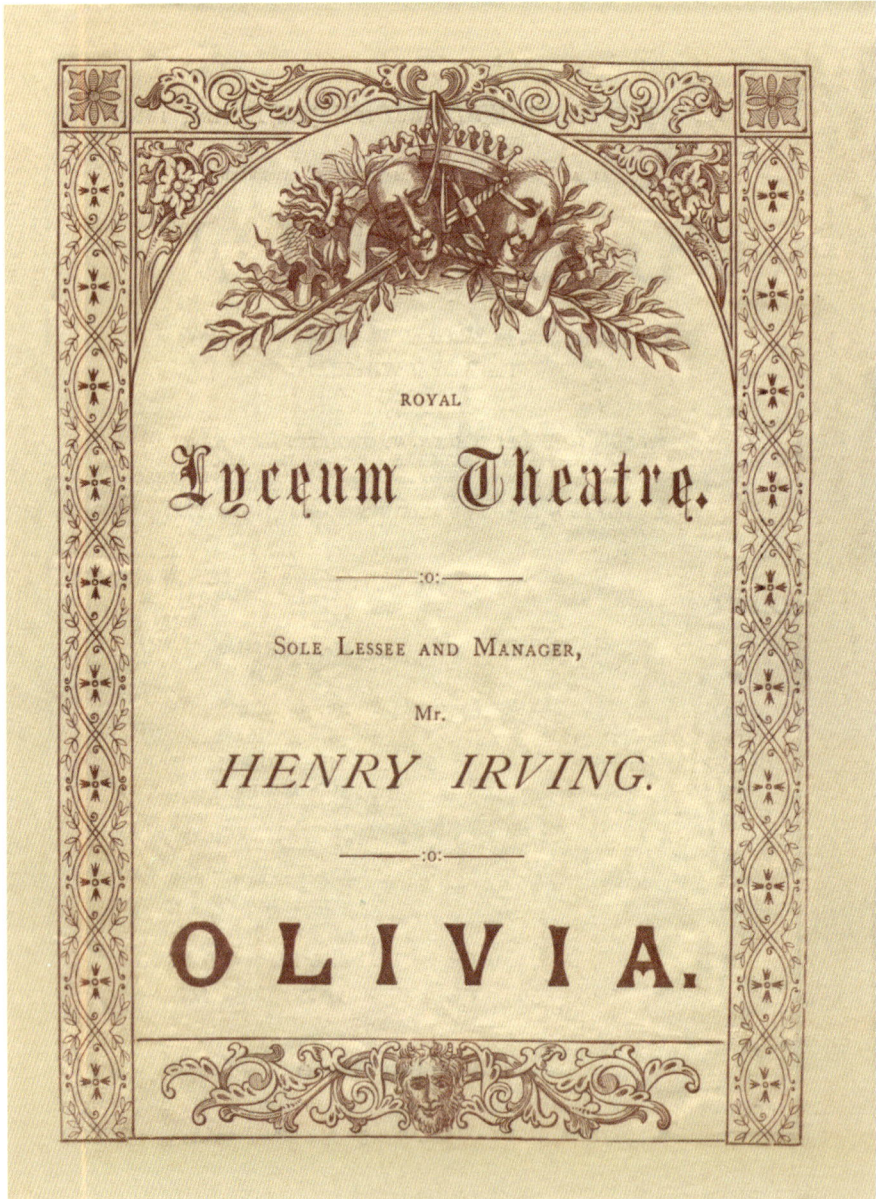

ROYAL

Lyceum Theatre.

:o:

SOLE LESSEE AND MANAGER,

Mr.

HENRY IRVING.

:o:

OLIVIA.

Mollie Vincent's programme for *Olivia*, which she saw
with her brother Will on July 22nd, 1885.

A tissue-paper napkin preserved by Mollie Vincent as a souvenir of her visit to the tea-room, which she described as 'very jolly and pretty'.

PROGRAMME

THE ANGLESEY HUNT.

Thursday, November 5th, 1885.

COMPTROLLER:
R. I. WYNNE JONES, ESQ.

DEPUTY-COMPTROLLER:
SIR R. H. WILLIAMS BULKELEY, BART.

PROGRAMME.

1	COUNTRY DANCE	..	..	
2	VALSE	..	..	Auf Wiederschen
3	POLKA	..	..	Toujours Buvait
4	VALSE	..	..	La Fête
5	LANCERS	..	..	Socerer
6	VALSE	..	..	The Cloister
7	POLKA	..	..	Drink, Puppy Drink
8	VALSE	..	..	Under the Stars
9	LANCERS	..	..	Mikado
10	GALOP	..	..	John Peel
11	POLKA	..	..	Spinning Wheel
12	LANCERS	..	..	Nell Gwynne
13	VALSE	..	..	Fairie Voices
14	POLKA	..	..	Chic
15	VALSE	..	Fleurs de St. Petersburg	
16	LANCERS	..	..	Iolanthe
17	VALSE	..	..	Mikado
18	POLKA	..	..	Black and Tan
19	VALSE	..	..	La Zingara
20	SIR ROGER			

R. JOHNSON'S BAND.

Mollie Vincent's dance programme for the final Anglesey Hunt Ball on Thursday November 5th, 1885.

✦ VAYNOL ✦ SCHOOL ✦ BANGOR ✦

EIGHTH ANNUAL CONCERT.

A GRAND CONCERT

WILL BE GIVEN IN THE ABOVE SCHOOL-ROOM,

ON FRIDAY EVENING, NOVEMBER 13th, 1885.

Chairman—W. M. PRESTON, Esq., VAYNOL.

CONDUCTOR:—MR. L. D. JONES, GARTH, BANGOR.

PROGRAMME.

Part First.

1.—PIANOFORTE SOLO	...	Miss Sackville West, Lime Grove.
2.—SONG	"Mignonette"	Mr O. Roberts (Eos Meirion).
3.—SONG	"A remembered voice"...	...Miss A. Williams, High Street, Bangor.
4.—SONG	"Y mynydd i mi"	Rev. F. Salt, Portdinorwic.
5.—SONG	...	Mr W. W. Ellis, Llanberis.
6.—DUETT	"I wandered in dreams"...	Miss A. Williams, Garth, and Mr O. Roberts.
7.—SONG	"The Bedouin love song"	Rev. D. Ffrangcon Davies, Conway.
8.—SONG	"London Bridge"	Mr F. E. Morgan, Normal College.
9.—COMIC SONG	..."Patrick mind the baby"...	Master F. H. Broome, Upper Bangor.
10.—SONG	"When the heart is young"	Miss A. Williams, Garth
11.—DUETT	"Mae Cymru'n barod, &c."...Messrs D. E. Williams & F. Jenkins, N. College.

Part Second.

12.—PIANOFORTE DUETT	...	Miss Sackville West and Miss Cecilie Sackville West.
13.—DIALOGUE (Nigger)	...	Master F. H. Broome and G. H. Higginson.
14.—SONG	"The Wolf"	Mr W. W. Ellis.
15.—SONG	"Neges y Blodeuyn"	...Miss A. Williams, Garth.
16.—SONG	"Good Bye"	Rev. D. Ffrangcon Davies.
17.—QUARTETTE	"Basso Profundo"	Normal College Quartette Party.
18.—SONG	"On wings of Song"	Miss Vincent, Treborth.
19.—SONG	"True till death"	Rev. F. Salt.
20.—SONG	"Katie's letter"	Miss A. Williams, Bangor.
21.—COMIC SONG	...	Mr H. Thomas, Llandegai.
22.—SONG	"Maid of the Mill"	Mr O. Roberts.
23.—FINALE	..."GOD SAVE THE QUEEN"...	

ACCOMPANISTS:—MRS. WHITE GRIFFITH, & MR. W. ROBERTS, UPPER BANGOR.

DOORS OPEN 6.30, TO COMMENCE AT 7 P.M. (PROMPT).

Admission:—*Chairs, 2s.; First Class, 1s.; Second Class, 6d.*

Proceeds in aid of the Day and Sunday School Funds.

Programme for a charity concert in which Mollie Vincent and some of her friends performed.

CAPTAIN COOK'S VOYAGES

ENTHUSIASTIC RECEPTION OF PLUM-PUDDING BY THE FRIENDLY LAPPS

Ye Plum Puddinge at ye Ancient Manor of Treborth

Ye bloted orientale magistrate in ye centre distributeth ye dainty in appropriate Sanskrite costume. To his right standeth Hugo [*Hugh*], ye wily solicitore who with spoone soliciteth a seconde helpe. Ye rite valient souldier Gustie standeth by with a look of truculente defiance in his eyes (observe ye eyes). Next to him ye young and unwise damsel GGWV [*Georgie*] becometh timorous and assumeth her wonted air of wistful thoughtfulness. On ye distributor's left Master and Mistress Lil rejoice to have secured eates for ye [*Lampeter*] schoole boyes to last many weeks; she enjoineth him not to eat thereof on ye slye. Sittinge on ye ground is MMV [*Mollie*] who has requested largesse of ye puddinge for charitable purposes. Havinge secured a large portion, she impaleth it on a two pronged driblet wire. Beside her sits Mistress Eva, ye proude and scornful beauté, who arrogantly disdaineth ye puddinge. Mistress Vincent [*Mother*] appeareth not, but from ye interior is heard wishing ye puddinge were deceased.

A Christmas card received in 1885 and used by Mollie Vincent as the basis of a whimsy which reveals something of the family's humour and individual characteristics. The figures are taken to represent those members of the family home for the holiday. Captain Cook is William Vincent who, when his training is complete, will go to India and become, initially, a magistrate.

A hand-drawn invitation from Miss Mary Pryce, a keen amateur musician who frequently held musical evenings at the canonry (now the Bangor Museum and Art Gallery).

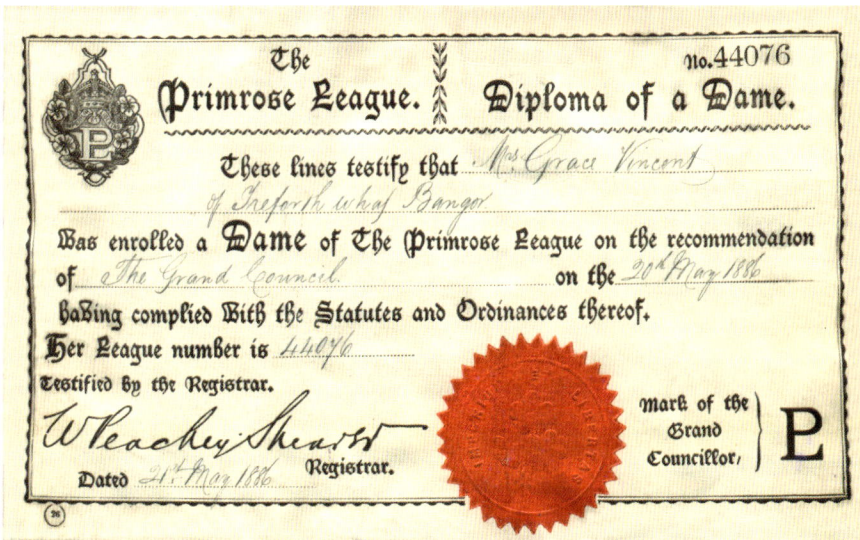

A 'diploma' recording Mrs Grace Vincent's enrolment as a Dame of the Primrose League. The League was formed in 1883 by a group of Conservative politicians led by Randolph Churchill, with the objective of upholding Crown, Church and Empire. The name was chosen as a tribute to Benjamin Disraeli whose favourite flower had been the primrose. Queen Victoria had placed a wreath of primroses on his grave on April 19th 1881.

The Old Flag & the New

The Royal Standard of the United Kingdom

of Great Britain and Ireland.

DO YOU WISH TO SEE IT MUTILATED

IN THIS FASHION?

IF NOT, RESIST HOME RULE
and the Dismemberment of the Empire.

RALLY ROUND THE OLD FLAG

GOD SAVE THE QUEEN!

C. TERRY & Co., Printers and Publishers, Little Denmark St., Soho, London.

A handbill, produced as part of the campaign against Gladstone's proposals for Irish Home Rule, preserved in the Diary.

Tuesday, April 6th:

"Davieses to tea. Georgie started for Beaumaris down the line as she lost her train.

On March 30th Lord Penrhyn had died at 80 years of age. Everyone was sorry because he did a great deal for the country. His funeral was celebrated today with some pomp." [*This was the first Lord Penrhyn, formerly Colonel E.G. Pennant.*]

Wednesday, April 7th:

"Mollie and Will went to the Rink to play tennis with the Sackville-Wests. We afterwards went and had tea at Lime Grove. Lionel showed his new tin birds which were hit but seldom, though many cartridges were wasted. We also played a beautiful new game which Mary [*Sackville-West*] loves."

Friday, April 9th:

"Mary and Cecilie Sackville-West and Lionel came to tea. Mollie made a member of Primrose League [*the Conservative Party association founded in 1883*]. Wyatts are gone, Norris came to see Will in Dublin in new check clothes, patent leather boots, square hat, lovely gloves and collar and tie in due proportion, altogether most prepossessing."

Saturday, April 10th:

"William made his equestrian effort on Dian. Crocuses found in the orchard and planted. Seeds planted in orchard garden."

Sunday, April 11th:

"Home rule scheme introduced by Gladstone and opposed by Chamberlain, Hartington, Trevelyan and Heneage. [*The Anti-Home Rule Coalition published the handbill 'Rally Round the Old Flag' which is preserved with the diary.*] The scheme is wild and scarcely satisfies the Irish while it causes the break up of the Liberal party."

[*The diary entries are now continued by Mollie Vincent.*]

Monday, April 12th:

"Day fine. Mollie went to Bangor [*for herself and Georgie*] to be registered at the college — then went on to Lime Grove for luncheon. Georgie went out for a ride with the Davieses. Will cleared the orchard path. Enid Davies and Jane Hughes came to tea. Gustie came back from Lampeter at half past six."

Easter Sunday, April 25th:

"Lil and Jack came down on Easter Eve. Hugh had been down [*from London*] two days. The weather was fine—we all went to the Cathedral."

Easter Monday, April 26th:

"Very fine all day. Hugh and Will went on a mountain walk with the Sackville-Wests."

Tuesday, April 27th:

"Hugh went back to London."

Wednesday, April 28th:

"Katie Davies' wedding. [*She was marrying her brother's brother-in-law, Dr S.N. Habershon of London.*] Very wet, cold and windy. In the morning Lil, Eva, Georgie, Will and Mollie went across the field and into the Ark [*Treborth Hall*] where all the girls came down in their bridesmaid dresses looking very pretty. When they had started, we went into the big drawing room where Katie was. She looked very nice and her dress was lovely, white slumped velvet over a satin petticoat covered with pearl and bead embroidery, tulle veil, sham orange blossom and diamond stars. It rained and blew very much as she got into the carriage. Then we came back and Mollie and Mother got changed and went to the breakfast. It was long, but there were no speeches, then at 3 o'clock Katie went away, the 3 Davies boys going with her to Bangor. Then in the evening, Eva, Georgie, Mollie, Will, Gus went in and we played games and had a very jolly supper, nicer than the breakfast."

Thursday, April 29th:

"Mary Watkin-Davies' wedding day. A great deal finer than the day before but still cold. Lil and Georgie went to see her pass [*through the Menai Bridge station*] and she looked very nice in a brown frock and the wedding was a great success in every way. In the evening Mollie and Mother dined at the [*Bishop's*] Palace. It was dull. Jessie Wynne-Jones and Miss Bruce [*two of the daughters of Lord Aberdare*] had lunched here. Lil, Georgie, Gustie and Will went into Treborth that evening. Jack went to Oxford the day before."

Friday, April 30th:

"The Ramsays came in the afternoon. In the evening Mother and Lil went to dinner at Mrs White Griffith's and afterwards to the *Elijah* concert at the Rink. They had a full orchestra, most of it members of the Halle band [*the Halle Orchestra of Manchester*]. Miss Eleanor Rees sang the contralto solos—she was very good-looking with lots of red hair. Ffrangcon Davies sang the Elijah part very well. Mollie went with the Barbers. Eva met Jack who came down from Oxford and came with him. Meg Wynne-Jones came for it. Mr Owen Evans appeared there too."

Saturday, May 1st:

"The Sackville-Wests came over to see Lil. So did Mr Owen Evans. We sat in the garden, it was fine."

Sunday, May 2nd:

"Will went away to Ireland."

Monday, May 3rd:

"Lil and Jack went away in the morning. In the afternoon Norris Wyatt and Hamilton Poole called and asked us to the theatrical and dance at Carnarvon." [*Hamilton Poole was a member of a Caernarfon legal family and a lieutenant in the 4th Battalion, Royal Welch Fusiliers.*]

Wednesday, May 5th:

"Edmund came down for Assizes. Fred Johnson came to stay here." [*Fred Johnson was the eldest son of the second marriage of the elder Rev. William Johnson. He was, therefore, a much younger half-brother of Mrs Grace Vincent.*]

Friday, May 7th and Saturday, May 8th:

[*Some members of the family attended the amateur dramatic productions at the Guildhall, Caernarfon. This was under the patronage of the High Sheriff, Sir Llewelyn Turner, Colonel Platt, and the Officers of the 4th Battalion, the Royal Welch Fusiliers. The band of the battalion provided the orchestra and proceeds were in aid of the National Lifeboat Association.*]

Sunday, May 9th:

"Mollie went on to the Davies Yacht for the first time, but there was no wind so didn't sail. Mother went to Bangor. Played tennis."

Monday, May 10th:

"Wet and cold."

UNDER THE PATRONAGE OF
The High Sheriff (Sir Llewelyn Turner); Col. Platt, and the Officers of the 4th Batt. R. W. Fusiliers.

GUILD HALL, CARNARVON.

TWO ENTERTAINMENTS

WILL BE GIVEN BY AN

AMATEUR DRAMATIC COMPANY,

Friday & Saturday, May 7th & 8th,
1886.

On Friday, the 7th, to commence with a Comedietta, in One Act, called

"BUBBLES,"

And to conclude with the Comedy, in Three Acts, entitled

"A LESSON IN LOVE."

On Saturday, the 8th, commencing with a Comedietta, entitled

"A HAPPY PAIR,"

And concluding with "A LESSON IN LOVE."

Orchestra :—Band of the 4th Batt. Royal Welsh Fusiliers.

PROCEEDS IN AID OF

THE NATIONAL LIFEBOAT INSTITUTION.

Tickets—2s., 1s., and 6d. Soldiers and Sailors in Uniform, Half-price to the Gallery. Doors open at 7.30; to commence at 8 p.m.

Stage Manager—MAJOR BLYTH.

PRINTED AT THE 'HERALD' OFFICE, CARNARVON.

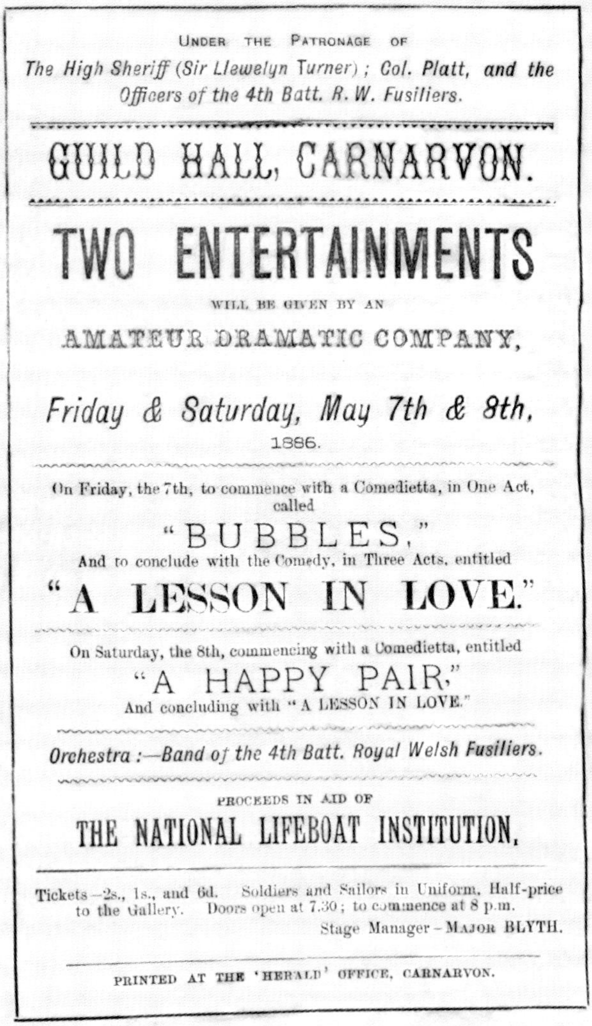

Tuesday, May 11th:

"Wetter and colder. Mollie and Gustie walked home from college in the rain."

Thursday, May 13th:

"Dora Watkin-Davies came from Rhyl where she had been staying with Mary [*her newly married sister, now Mrs Haywood-Brown, of Sywell House, Rhyl.*]"

Friday, May 14th:

"Day fine but cold. Mollie went to Bangor, first to a lecture then to call at the Hugheses'. After that went to the Cathedral and saw the new window given by Mrs Symes in memory of the Dean [*Edwards*]. It was all in except the left-hand round light under the big centre light. After that Mollie went to Penrhyn Castle, was taken into the park by one of the Pennants, went a short drive and then in to tea. They were all very kind and the room was lovely like a dream, and the tea was good. We talked about the LMHA and the new hostel for women going to be built for the college. The Sackville-Wests had been at home and Mother became a Dame of the Primrose League. The kitchen was whitewashed and looks clean. Heard from Hugh."

Saturday, May 15th:

"The white pony returned after wanderings that had lasted three weeks, she appeared none the worse. Tennis in the afternoon. Dora [*Watkin-Davies*] and Fred v. Georgie and Mollie. Gustie played cricket, scored 8."

Sunday, May 16th:

"Did not go to church in the morning, too wet. Fred and Gus went though. Went in the afternoon, rather cold. Georgie and MMV walked back, met the white pony in the Park, again running away for pastures new, returned it to top field where it was bitten by Ruff, doubtless from a worthy motive if the thing could have been properly analysed — no one tried to analyse and she was recalled unblessed. G [Georgie] wrote to Hugh, Mother to Will, MMV to Lil, and so Sunday ended."

Monday, May 17th:

"Very wet day. Dora went away."

Tuesday, May 18th:

"Mother and Mollie went to Bangor and called on the Hugheses of Bryn Menai, Mrs White Griffith, [*and the*] Hindes — new people, Irish, don't expect to like them much. Then on the McKinstrys, afterwards on Mrs Evans of the Canonry. On our way home, went to say goodbye to Mrs Davies and Mary [*at Treborth Hall*]. Had tea there. Enid and Trixie Davies were here to tea and tennis. Mary came over to say goodbye to the others."

Colonel Henry Platt of Gorddinog, Llanfairfechan, commanding officer of the Caernarfon Militia (4th Battalion Royal Welch Fusiliers). He became Mayor of Bangor and was a prominent member of the Conservative Party. The Platt family were owners of the company of that name based in Oldham, then the world's largest manufacturers of cotton-spinning machinery, with extensive overseas interests, especially in Asia. (University of Wales, Bangor)

Sir Llewelyn Turner, founder of Turner and Allanson, Solicitors, Caernarfon. He became Mayor of Caernarfon, Deputy Constable of Caernarfon Castle and High Sheriff of the county. He was also Chairman of the Caernarfon Victoria Harbour Trust and was closely involved with the Caernarfon lifeboat. In addition, he was Chairman of the North Wales Narrow Gauge Railway Company and Commodore of the Royal Welsh Yacht Club. (Gwynedd Archives)

Wednesday, May 19th:

"Wet day, Mollie went to lecture, then got ready things to go to dinner party at Plas Tirion [*home of Mr Hugh Roberts, solicitor and clerk to the Caernarfon magistrates*]. Eva and Mollie started at 5.15 from here. Met at Llanrug by dogcart, drove to the house, found some fuss and strange waiters. Dressed, came down, met a lot of Bedients, also some militia officers—Colonels Platt, Wayne, and Craig; Mr Hamilton Poole, Mr Cadogan (eyes half shut), Mr Hogg (like a little pig—Eva says pigling); Mr Owen Evans of Broom Hall [*Pwllheli*], Mr Llewelyn Turner. Dinner long, excellent and most expensive." ['*Bedients' was perhaps the Vincent family term for lawyers who would end their letters 'Your obedient servant'.*]

Thursday, May 20th:

"Wet day, very wet. Eva and Mollie left Plas Tirion at 11 in the morning without incident except playing with the two fat little girls of the house. Came home and said many happy returns of the day to Georgie. The day was uniformly dull and wet, not nice for a birthday. Heard from Ted, Babs had measles, uneasy."

Friday, May 21st:

"Fine day. Gustie went to the Sackville-Wests for tennis. Fred [*Johnson, still staying at Treborth*] went to Bangor to get powder and shot. Telegram came from Edmund to say Babs was worse and asking Mother to go. New housemaid came — Margaret."

Saturday, May 22nd:

"Mother went by 8 o'clock train to London. Day fine, Gustie went to a cricket match at Carnarvon. Fred shot rabbits. He and Gustie went to Penrhyn Hall in the evening. The Ramsays and Miss Homfrey came for a few minutes to ask about Babs."

Sunday, May 23rd:

"Drove to Cathedral, heard Bishop Reichel preach. Splendid sermon, big congregation. Heard from Mother that she had arrived safely and Babs was better."

Monday, May 24th:

"Fine day. Sat in the garden all afternoon and heard the cuckoo. Gustie and Mollie saw the telegraph boy and Gustie ran to get the telegram. Edmund and

Babs' little girl was born. Mollie ran to tell Georgie and Eva, they told Owen, he put up the flag and drank the baby's health. [*The baby daughter, Violet Mary, was born at Ted's home, 4 Fulham Park Road.*] Fred gone to Liverpool. New kitchen maid came from Treiorwerth."

Tuesday, May 25th:

"Wet day — no news from London."

Wednesday, May 26th:

"Mollie went to Lime Grove to a dinner party, met Bishop Reichel, stayed the night. Fred came back from Liverpool."

Thursday, May 27th:

"Mollie came back from Lime Grove, drenching day."

Friday, May 28th:

"Mollie went to Bangor. Sat up to half past one waiting for Mother and Hugh who arrived, heard all the news about the baby. Cold day."

Saturday, May 29th:

"Fine day. The McKinstrys came to tennis in the afternoon. All felt rather tired after the sitting up at night."

Monday, May 31st:

"Fred went to Llaniestyn. The Sackville-Wests came to tea. Day very grey and cold."

Wednesday, June 2nd:

"Hartley Cook [*a young member of the family of Ted's wife*] came, jolly little boy who talked about pirates before he had been two minutes in the house. Very wet day."

Thursday, June 3rd, Ascension day,:

"Mr Owen Evans came to dinner and showed us the plans for the new church at Glanadda [*Bangor – St David's Church*]. Mother went twice to Bangor that day."

Friday, June 4th:

"The Bishop of Meath and Miss Reichel called and were very nice. Day fine. Mollie had gone to Carnarvon that afternoon. Hartley built ports in the pool all day."

Saturday, June 5th:

"Mother started in the morning with Mr Owen Evans to Lampeter. Fine day. Mollie went a long walk in the fields with Hartley in the morning, Eva went with him in the afternoon to put the dogs in the water. Georgie built more ports in the afternoon. Gustie went to a cricket match."

Sunday, June 6th:

"We drove to the Cathedral, heard Bishop Reichel preach. The church was very full, the anthem was 'King All Glorious'. Day very fine. Georgie and Mollie had tight new frocks. Had good news of Babs."

Monday, June 7th:

"Miss Reichel came to luncheon. Sat out all afternoon. Georgie lunched at Lime Grove, drove back with Cecilie. Mollie went to stay at Lime Grove. Fred came back from Llaniestyn."

Tuesday, June 8th:

"Miss Mary Pritchard called. Mollie went to tea at the Reichels' and then on to tennis at the College. Met the Trechmanns there—very nice people. [*Mr Trechmann was lecturer in German at the University College of North Wales.*] Heard from Mother who was enjoying herself very much."

Wednesday, June 9th:

"Mollie still at Lime Grove. Hartley and Georgie came over and they sailed boats in the pool [*on the River Cegin, just above Port Penrhyn at Lime Grove*]."

Thursday, June 10th:

"Mollie came home, found the family well, Fred as usual."

Friday, June 11th:

"Rain. Mr Dodd to dinner, nice boy who plays very well."

Saturday, June 12th:

"Fred went away in the morning. Hartley and Mollie went to meet Aunt Anne at half past four, found her looking very well and nice as usual, asked about the ladies. Then Mother came home at half past six bringing us all presents and we heard all about Jack and Lil and Mother's visit."

Sunday, June 13th:

"Cathedral. Fine day. Heard of poor Mr Roberts of Plas Tirion's death today."

Monday, June 14th:

"Carnarvon horse show. Dian got highly commended. It rained all day. Gustie was on a mountain walk with the Sackville-Wests, came home in all Lionel's clothes."

Tuesday, June 15th:

"The Sackville-Wests came to tennis day. Blowy and horrid."

Wednesday, June 16th:

"Mollie and Georgie went to Bangor for a lecture."

Thursday, June 17th:

"Norris Wyatt appeared and stayed the night, he was very nice."

Friday, June 18th:

"Violet Mary Vincent was baptised at Fulham. Her godmothers and godfather are Minnie Leach [*Babs' sister*], Mollie and Hugh. Mollie saw Mary Cotterill on her way home."

Saturday, June 19th:

"Heard from Babs about the christening. Heard from Lil, heard from Aunt Mary Needham that the troop ship *Jumna* was come into Plymouth. Colonel Thomas and cousin Madge came this afternoon. Edmund's white pony was sold. Eva and Aunt Anne went to Bangor. Heard Aunt George [*wife of Archdeacon Wynne-Jones*] had had to go to Droitwich."

Sunday, June 20th:

"Thanksgiving service in the Cathedral as it was the Queen's Accession, the forty ninth year of her reign."

Tuesday, June 22nd:

"Very wet day but the German people called Trechmann came and spent the afternoon in spite of the weather, bar that they came when we didn't expect them, they were nice."

Wednesday, June 23rd:

"Gustie played a cricket match and got a smack on his finger, no other incident worth recording."

Thursday, June 24th:

"Miss Williams and her sister the nun came to call, they were both nice, the nun looked odd, no gloves and a very large gold cross. We sent off a box of white pinks to the Northern Hospital, Liverpool."

Friday, June 25th:

"Nothing happened."

Sunday, June 27th:

"Everyone went to church bar Mollie. Fine day, fires given up for good. Hugh dined with Katie Habershon up in London on the 26th. [*Katie Habershon née Davies of Treborth Hall, lived with her surgeon husband at 88 Harley Street.*] Will and Hugh both coming home this week."

[*The next entry covering the period from the end of June to August 2nd is written by Evangeline (Eva) Vincent.*]

June

"The rest of this month was not very interesting or at least any points of interest are forgotten."

July

"Hugh and Will came home. Hugh passed his Final Exam and got a Second Class in his Honours Exam which might have been better but then again might have been worse. Will went to Lampeter and then on to Brecon to play a series of cricket matches for the Old Breconians. Mollie went to stay at Llandwyn with Meg Wynne-Jones and had a good time of it. The man King stayed here during the latter half of the month. Georgie stayed at Lampeter and has not yet returned to the ancestral halls."

August 1st (Sunday).

"We went to Llanfairpwll to church in the new boat which we have bought from the representatives of the late Hugh Roberts. Gus and Hugh were much smitten by the charms of the Morgan girls [*daughters of Captain Morgan of Plas Coed Mor*] who are pretty. Carter [*legal colleague of Hugh's and future partner in Carter Vincent and Co., solicitors*] walked [*the 7 miles*] over from Carnarvon in the afternoon and stayed for supper."

August 2nd (Monday)

"King, Hugh and Gus rowed [*the 6 miles*] to Beaumaris as Hugh wanted to see Aunt Louisa on business. King and Gus played tennis with Dora and Violet [*Ramsay*] who came back with them as far as Garth to the peril of the boat and its inmates."

[*When Mollie Vincent returned, she continued the diary with retrospective accounts of her visit to Llanddwyn.*]

Thursday, July 29th:

"Mr Owen Evans lunched here. Mollie and Mr Owen Evans settled to get up a memorial to the late Dean at Glanadda Church. Meg Wynne and Mollie started for Llanddwyn. They went [*probably by train from the tiny Treborth Halt station*] to Carnarvon, then crossed over to Anglesey by the Tan-y-foel ferry, [*where they were met and taken*] on by car [*small carriage*] to Newborough. Drove on then by a car across the sand to Llanddwyn, found house ready."

The Pilots' Cottages at Llanddwyn, where Mollie Vincent and Meg Wynne-Jones spent a brief holiday and 'had a good time of it'.

Saturday, July 31st:

"Mother and Mr King came over [*to Newborough and Llanddwyn*] with Hugh and Gus. Rather rough day. Meg and Mollie very glad to see them. Gave them tea. Went to wishing well." [*This is the well of St Dwynwen, the Welsh patron saint of lovers.*]

Wednesday, August 4th:

"Mollie came back from Llanddwyn. Uncle William [*Johnson*] had been here. Mollie came back across Malltraeth marsh to Bodorgan [*to take the train back to Menai Bridge station*]."

Thursday, August 5th:

"Carnarvon regatta. Mollie started in the boat with Gustie and Mr King. Wind too high to get on. Turned back, found Colonel Thomas and cousin Madge. Hugh and Mollie walked down and saw Colonel Thomas' new horse."

Saturday, August 7th:

"All the Sackville-Wests to tennis and tea, a reconciliation visit after a row with them, all rather fun. Mollie, Hugh, Gus and Mr King went that evening to the circus. Hugh stopped a fight between two drunken men. We loved the lions at the circus, the boys laughed at the clowns' jokes, they were low (both are meant)."

Monday, August 9th:

"The Ramsays to luncheon, Dora and Violet, also Lionel and Mr Leach. Mr Fairchild and Bertie Sackville-West came in the afternoon; it was very fine and a great success. Mother, Mollie and Hugh went to the Primrose League dinner that evening at the Penrhyn Hall. It was supposed to begin at 9 o'clock, did begin at 8. Lord Penrhyn sent his son to preside instead of himself. We thought him rather a dull youth, but he didn't manage very badly. There wasn't much to eat and the drinks were dear. Speeches long and dull. Mr Swetenham looked very pleasant and seemed to make jokes but they weren't really funny at all. Mr Kenyon was a wee bit better, more jokes but longer … a parson spoke in Welsh … we sang 'The Fine Old English Gentleman', 'Gwlad Gwlad'['*Hen wlad fy Nhadau*'] and many other excellent songs. Finally we all sang 'God Save the Queen' with immense fervour and came away at 1 o'clock."

Thursday, August 12th:

"Mr Griffith Williams came to see Dian, who was already sold to Mr Brocklebank for £40. [*William Brocklebank, whose home, just outside Menai Bridge town, overlooked the Menai Strait, was a member of the well-known shipping line family.*] Mollie went to Treiorwerth that day. Mother, Georgie, Mr King and Hugh went out with the Davieses in the *Aeolia*. Day wet."

Friday, August 13th:

"Mollie still at Treiorwerth. They had a large garden party there. Hugh at work at his new office."

Saturday, August 14th:

"Denis Cotterill [*the 5-year-old son of their second cousin Mary, née Wynne-Jones*] came back with Mollie. Dr Prytherch came to see Eva, said she was very weak but that he could put her right. The Davieses came to tennis in the afternoon."

Monday, August 16th:

"Mr and Mrs Thomas to luncheon. Expected the Griffithses of Gaerwen. Day wet. Mr Thomas brought his memorial of the late Dean for Mother to look at the first pages. Heard today by telegram of Mrs Cook's death [*mother-in-law of Ted*]."

Wednesday, August 18th:

"Mollie went with Mother to call on the Edwardses at Bangor, also on Alice Greg Hughes, and Mrs Rowlands. Came back to find Annie Barber and Mrs Walter Barber's little girl here. She is very pretty."

Friday, August 20th:

"Dora and Frank [*Watkin-Davies*] and Tom Makin came to spend the day. Eva was very ill. Mollie had spent the day before with the Sackville-Wests going to Penmon. Georgie, Gus, Hugh and Mr King went to a tennis party at Trecastell. Mr King went out with the Davieses to Beaumaris regatta. The Davieses raced their yacht. The day was miserable because Eva was so ill. Had Dr Prytherch twice and Dr Williams for consultation. The Davieses were very nice and it was delightful having Frank and Dora. After they were gone Eva became worse. At 12 o'clock Hugh drove Mr King to the station and brought back Dr Gray Edwards [*Dr Henry Gray Edwards, MB, of 274 High Street, Bangor*]. Eva was then slightly better."

Saturday, August 21st:

"Eva was a little better. The Sackville-Wests had unfortunately been asked so we did not put them off. Day dull and wet, but the Sackville-Wests were awfully nice and jolly. Mrs Davies came to see us and Trixie brought in fruit for Eva."

Tuesday, August 24th:

"Gustie gone to Ireland. Mrs John Edwards and her little girl came to tea. Eva better."

Wednesday, August 25th:

"Will and Georgie went to an 'At Home' at the Davieses' [*Treborth Hall*]."

Thursday, August 26th:

"Carnarvon Tennis Tournament. Georgie, Hugh, Will and Harry Griffith all entered from this house. None of them was successful. Day most miserable, rain and wind."

Friday, August 27th:

"Georgie and Mollie went to Bangor to buy some things for Lil. Hugh and Will went to Carnarvon to finish the tournament. When Georgie and Mollie came back they found Lionel and Charlie [*Sackville-West*]. A long wet day but not horrid."

[*Entries for the remainder of August and September 1st are in the hand of Georgie Vincent.*]

Saturday, August 28th:

"Mollie went to Bardsey (in the Mayor of Bangor's steamer) with the Menai Society. The day was fine but windy, most of the members were sea-sick, otherwise the expedition was a success. [*Bardsey Island, at the northern limit of Cardigan Bay, was a round trip from Bangor of approximately 90 miles.*] Gustie came back from Ireland. Will and Georgie brought the dogs down to the covert."

Sunday, August 29th:

"The Mam, Eva and Mollie stayed away from church, the Mam with Eva, and Mollie to pack her clothes for Ireland, where she went by the 12.40 train to stay with the Scovells. Hugh and Georgie walked to the Cathedral where they heard 'As pants the Heart' beautifully sung. Will and Gustie rowed themselves over to Llanfairpwll church [*opposite Treborth Uchaf on the Anglesey side of the Menai Strait*]."

Monday, August 30th:

"In the morning Georgie and Gustie went to Bangor by the 10.05 train to do some shopping. The Mam and Eva came to meet them at the station on their way back. Eva looks a great deal better today and the doctor says she is getting on very well. In the afternoon Will, Georgie and Gustie went to a tennis party at Plas Cadnant [*Llandegfan*] where there were a great many people (principally from Beaumaris). The tennis ground was good but there were no very good sets played. Mr Hogg, an old TCD friend of Hugh's came to dinner." [*W. Hogg, from Kendal in the Lake District, played rugby for Trinity College, Dublin, with Hugh Vincent.*]

Tuesday, August 31st:

"Will and Gustie cut and marked the tennis ground. Mary Sackville-West and Miss Wyatt came in the afternoon and took Eva for a drive which she enjoyed and which did her good. They came back afterwards and had some tea and tennis. The tennis court plays well this year."

Wednesday, September 1st:

"Had letters from Mollie and Lil this morning. Mary Davies came over in the morning to see Eva and to ask us to their 'At Home' in the afternoon. Will, Georgie and Gustie went to the 'At Home' which was a great success and most decidedly the best one that has been given about here this year. While they were away, Major and Mrs Ruck came to call and were much liked by the Mam and Eva (particularly Mrs Ruck)." [*Major Ruck was later made a Colonel and Chief Constable of Carnarvonshire.*]

[*The narrative now reverts to Mollie*].

Tuesday, September 7th:

"Gustie and Mollie went to Beaumaris to go to a pic-nic given by the Ramsays. There was an accident in which one carriage was completely broken up. Gustie, Fanny, Dora and Miss Bourn were thrown out but no one was much hurt except Aunt Louisa who was much bruised."

Wednesday, September 8th:

"Mr and Mrs Leach and Tom came and spent the day which was very wet. Lionel and Charlie Sackville-West came and after the Leaches were gone, we went out nutting in the covert."

Thursday, September 9th:

"The day was very windy, not good for the boys' shooting. They had Lionel and Mr Hugh Rowlands to shoot with, but had not so good a day as they ought to have had because of the wind."

Friday, September 10th:

"The day was fine but it had been wet for more or less a week so the Tennis ground was in a soak, but we had a lot of people and the afternoon passed off very well. Frank Watkin-Davies appeared unexpectedly and was as usual delightful. Will came back from Pentraeth bringing Harry with him. Heard that Gus had passed his prelim." [*The Preliminary Examination for the Army held on 25th and 26th August 1886, which he had sat in Ireland.*]

Saturday, September 11th:

"Mr Hogg [*presumably a different Mr Hogg from the gentleman who visited on 30th August, and perhaps an official of the London and North Western Railway Company*] came from Crewe to look at the Tube [*Britannia Tubular Bridge*] and us. Charlie and Bertie Sackville-West came to dinner. Bertie sang a song very prettily."

Sunday, September 12th:

"Cathedral in the morning, rained all day. Mr Hogg went back to Crewe."

Monday, September 13th:

"Gus and Mollie went to Cadnant to a Tennis party which was rather fun. Mr Jones the curate of Menai Bridge stayed to dinner."

Tuesday, September 14th:

"Boys went out conger fishing in the morning and shooting in the afternoon."

Wednesday, September 15th:

"Gustie and Lloyd shot all day. Trixie [*the ten-year-old youngest daughter of the Davieses of Treborth Hall*] came in to find Georgie and found her in bed with a cold. Eva a little better. Harry [*Griffith*] went away today. Mrs Rowlands and Miss Rowlands came to say goodbye before sailing for India, both very good-looking."

Thursday, September 16th:

"Llewie Wynne-Jones suddenly appeared in the afternoon and stayed. Cecilie, back from her cruise, came to tea. Hamilton Poole and his sister called."

Saturday, September 18th:

"Will Wynne-Jones rowed up from Carnarvon with a very small curate and another man and had luncheon, after which he rushed off to Bangor to a meeting about the [*University College of North Wales*] girls' hostel. The boys shot all morning. Went out in the boat in the afternoon. After tea we had Tennis."

Monday, September 20th:

"We had a 'Tennis'. Very fine day. Party was a success, everyone was nice, there were lots of men. Llewie left us for Treiorwerth. Will Wynne-Jones was here, very jolly, Major and Mrs Ruck were here from Carnarvon and lots of other people. Hugh up in London with Lionel. Harry Griffith and Hamilton Poole stayed to dinner. Georgie's cold better, Eva better."

Tuesday, September 21st:

"Windy cold day. Dr Prytherch to see Eva and Georgie, says they are both on the mend. Gustie went out with Mr Assheton Smith's otter hounds, he had a good day. Hugh came down from London, having enjoyed himself very much. Will and Mollie went down to the covert."

Wednesday, September 22nd:

"Cold day but bright. Mollie, Georgie, Gustie and Will played Tennis in the wind. Edith Davies and Jane Hughes called. Georgie and Mollie went out for a walk. Will and Gustie watched for wood pigeon which never came! Mother heard from Babs this morning. Allan Ramsay arrived to dinner having ridden on his Tricycle from Porthmadog — took from half past two to half past six. Will's chickens ill with the gapes."

Thursday, September 23rd:

"Cold day. Mollie sent money off to the LHMA. Had bad news of Jim Johnson [*son of Mother's brother, Canon William Johnson of Llaniestyn*]. Day passed without incident, we played tennis."

Friday, September 24th:

"Fine day without sun. Had some people to our last tennis party of this year. It didn't go badly, we're glad it's over."

Saturday, September 25th:

"Wet, all day. Will and Gus worked the ferret and bought a new one. Will took both ferrets with him to Pentraeth [*on a visit to Harry Griffith*]. Sent Lil's things off. Annie and Alice [*Barber of Penrallt, Bangor*] came and had tea. Alice told us all about her voyage from Australia. [*Alice had returned on the* Hampshire *a month or so earlier, from a nine-month trip to Australia for the benefit of her husband, Dr Greg Hughes' health*.] Will Wynne-Jones came to dinner, went away at seven thirty."

Sunday, September 26th:

"Eva drove to the Cathedral for the first time since her illness. It was a fine day. When we got back, Will and Harry had walked over from Pentraeth; they went back that evening. The Dean preached at the 'Tin'."

Tuesday, September 28th:

"Mother, Georgie, Gustie and Mollie went out in the *Aeolia*. We had a nice sail until it began to rain. Katie had come home the day before, we saw her for a moment. When we got back we found the Sackville-Wests had been here and that Mr Perry Ringwood [*another friend of Hugh Vincent's from TCD, where he was a prizeman in International Law*] had called and was at the George Hotel. So Mother sent the dog cart for him and he came back and stayed for a few days. Hugh came back from Shrewsbury where he had been with Aunt Louisa and Ella [*Ramsay*] about trustee business. Played whist."

Wednesday, September 29th:

"Mr Ringwood went to Carnarvon with Hugh to look at his office, then in the afternoon, Georgie, Gus and Mollie took him down to the covert which looked very jolly and we pretended to look for nuts and got about 10. When we got back, Will and Harry had arrived from Pentraeth. We danced in the evening."

The gaff-rigged cutter *Aeolia* owned by the Davies family of Treborth Hall. The boat had a permanent crew of four. Members of the Vincent family were regularly invited on sailing excursions on the Menai Straits. (Sir Timothy Colman)

139

Thursday, September 30ᵗʰ:

"Will Wynne-Jones came to luncheon. The boys ferreted all afternoon."

Friday, October 1ˢᵗ:

"Pouring wet day as is usual on a 1st. Will, Gustie and Harry shot all morning but not with much success. Mr Ringwood went away at 12 o'clock. The girls' hostel was opened at Bangor." [*This was the first residence hall built by the new University College. It was situated at the lower end of the High Street, within two hundred yards of the college buildings.*]

Saturday, October 2ⁿᵈ:

"A lovely day. The boys shot all morning, then Georgie, Mollie, Will and Harry went out for a sail in the *Aeolia*. It was very lovely and they all enjoyed it very much. Hugh had a case at Carnarvon for the Board of Guardians before the magistrates. He managed very well and won his case."

[*A newspaper report of Hugh Vincent's case, which may well have been his first court appearance, is preserved in the diary.*]

"On Saturday, before Captain Wynn Griffith and other magistrates, Thomas Jones, Carreg House, Newborough, was summoned at the instance of the Carnarvon Guardians for refusing to contribute towards the maintenance of his father, who was in receipt of 4 shillings weekly as out-relief. Mr Vincent, who prosecuted, said that the defendant who was a master mariner, receiving six pounds monthly, lived in his own house, was possessed of three others, and no children dependent on him. The Board wanted him to contribute half a crown weekly but he offered only eighteenpence. Mr Allanson, who appeared for the defendant, said there were other sons equally able to contribute. It was not right that this son should be specially selected, because there appeared to have been some quarrel between the Guardians of Newborough parish and the defendant's wife. Mr Ellis, the district relieving officer, said that one of the sons was in Australia and the other a mate on a small schooner and had four children. Mr Menzies: I am astonished that the case should be defended. Why should the ratepayers be called upon to support a man whose son is earning six pounds a month? The bench confirmed the order."

"Hugh and Gustie played a football match which they won. Heard from Babs. Heard from Lil yesterday. Cousin Meta [*Bankes-Price*] was here to luncheon. Lionel and Cecilie were here to tea. We had bad news from Llaniestyn about poor Jim; he seems worse."

Sunday, October 3rd:

"Went to Cathedral. Eva better, she went to church. Day warm. Hugh and Harry Griffith rowed over to Llanfairpwll Church. Mollie went to the 'Tin'."

Monday, October 4th:

"Very hot day, very sultry with hot wind, all the fires had to be put out. The boys ferreted all day. Lionel was here. Allan Ramsay came to luncheon on his tricycle. Harry Griffith went home this afternoon, much regretted by everyone. Katie Habershon came in to tea and sang the 'Song of the Wren' by Sullivan very well. Lionel stayed to dinner and at half past ten it is still as hot as it can be. Gustie began his term at the college. Georgie has entered for her German Lectures Intermediate, as she passed her Matriculation last time."

Tuesday, October 5th:

"Will and Lionel went out after the hounds, had a good run, came back, had tea and shot for an hour. The day was very hot until five o'clock when it began to rain and drenched everyone who was out."

Wednesday, October 6th:

"It rained all day and we had the threshing machine. Twenty four sacks in all, which was a bad yield."

Thursday, October 7th:

"Lionel came over in the morning to ferret with Will. Hugh joined them at luncheon time. The day was fine. Mother, Georgie and Mollie took them down their tea and it was quite lovely. Mollie and Will went back with Lionel, had tea at Lime Grove and then went to an entertainment at the Penrhyn Hall where, amongst other things, they saw *The Vanishing Lady*. Will and Mollie walked home afterwards."

Friday, October 8th:

"Fine day. Bethel Roberts came to Treborth and went with Will out shooting at Vodol and Bryniau — five pheasants and four partridges. Also a brace of partridges out of the cobbly [*a rocky ridge covered in gorse*] in the back field. Hugh went out with one Morgan of Bryngwyn and killed 6 brace. Bethel Roberts stayed to dinner. Georgie went to college."

Saturday, October 9th:

"Day fairly fine. Mollie and Georgie went out blackberrying near Llanfair and got some blackberries and came back in the boat with Will and Lionel who had been out with the Marquis' hounds. There was a very good run. Mollie saw the death and saw the men were miles behind. We were some way behind too, a quarter of a mile or so. Lionel came to dinner and smoked afterwards. Gus and Hugh played football for the Carnarvon Wanderers against the Carnarvon training college [*later St Mary's College, Bangor*] and lost after a poor and wet match."

Sunday, October 10th:

"Went to the Cathedral and heard the Bishop of Meath preach."

Monday, October 11th:

"Gustie began his French lessons with M. Jaques. [*This was presumably Monsieur Jacquet B.A. (Paris) who advertised in the* North Wales Chronicle*. He gave private lessons in French, Latin and Greek at his home in Garth Road, Bangor.*] Mr Bankes-Price came to stay for the 'Retreat' at Bangor. Eva and Will went to Ireland."

Tuesday, October 12th:

"Very wet day. Mother bought some sheep."

Wednesday, October 13th:

"Mary, Cecilie and Lionel Sackville-West came but only for a little time as their little dog was killed in coming here and they were very sorry, so were we. Georgie went to lecture. Mr Bankes-Price went home, apparently tired of retreating."

Thursday, October 14th:

"Gustie and Hugh shot all afternoon and had a very good day's sport: 12 rabbits, 3 pheasants, 3 partridges. Georgie and Mollie went out blackberrying. Mr Dan Lewis came to call and had some tea. [*The Reverend Daniel Lewis Lloyd, Will's headmaster at Brecon was in Bangor on Church affairs. He was to become the Bishop of Bangor four years later in 1890.*] Trixie came in the morning to ask Mother and the boys to dinner and Georgie to go to some cooking lessons."

Friday, October 15th:

"Wet day. Georgie went to a cooking lesson at Menai Bridge with the Davieses. Mollie went to Bangor and bought a pound lamp for William Williams and a 2/11ᵈ one for this house. Mother and Mollie in the afternoon went up to the 'Tin' and decorated for the 'Harvest Home'."

Monday, October 18th:

"'Harvest Home' at the 'Tin'. Very disagreeable day all through. Bad news from Treiorwerth [*concerning the health of the 82-year-old Archdeacon John Wynne-Jones*]."

Tuesday, October 19th:

"Hugh had a very bothering day in Carnarvon. Mollie went to luncheon at the Sackville-Wests'. The little Thomases were there and acted a play invented by themselves. The town was covered with flags because it was Miss Kathleen Douglas Pennant's wedding day. [*The eldest daughter of the new Lord Penrhyn married Col. The Hon. Evelyn Boscawen, son and heir of Viscount Falmouth at St Paul's Church, Knightsbridge, London.*] It was a very horrid day here. Heard from Will this morning, not a very good account of Eva."

Wednesday, October 20th:

"Katie Habershon [*née Davies*] and Mary Davies came to luncheon. Mr Habershon was asked but was ill. Georgie went to a lecture. Mollie went in the afternoon to Carnarvon to stay with Jessie Wynne-Jones."

Thursday, October 21st:

"Ffrangcon Davies spent the day here, he sang well."

Friday, October 22nd:

"Pretty good news of Uncle John [*Archdeacon Wynne-Jones*], not good of poor Jim Johnson. Mollie came back from Carnarvon. Mother had entertained a lot of callers. Day fine. Ted arrived from London at 1 a.m., Mother and Hugh sat up for him."

Saturday, October 23rd:

"Mother heard from Mr Thomas this morning that the late Dean's relation wished him to discontinue the life of the late Dean which he was writing. He was naturally much annoyed. Mollie had a long account from Lil of herself. Ted was made to make a full and true account of [*his daughter*] Violet, alias, 'Bunting'. He says she sings 'gee ung gee-gaw' when she's very pleased. Ted and Gustie shot all morning. Ted, Hugh and Gustie played football all afternoon, they were all three very tired. Mollie and Georgie drove with the Sackville-West girls blackberrying, it was a jolly day though the blackberries weren't much of a success. We came back to tea and light cakes. Found Mr and Mrs Rathbone just going away."

[*Entry by Ted Vincent.*]

Sunday, October 24th:

"Owen didn't want to drive to Cathedral; said the mare's shoes were too old. Ted thwarted him by making him help to carry the boat down to and up from the water. Mollie, Hugh, Georgie walked to Cathedral: results better than might have been expected. Both Mollie and GG [*Georgie*] wore their stripes and looked monstrous fine. Partridge for supper."

[*Entries from October 25th to November 4th are by Georgie Vincent.*]

Monday, October 25th:

"Ted went away by the 3.40 train. Georgie walked with him to Bangor and then on to a German lecture at the college. The Mam and Mollie went to dinner at the Sackville-Wests' to meet Lord Powis. Hugh missed his train from Carnarvon so Gus and Georgie had a head à head dinner."

Tuesday, October 26th:

"East wind day, many visitors. Edith Davies [*fourth daughter of Richard Davies of Treborth Hall*] came in to announce her engagement to Mr Russell Colman [*of the Norwich family of mustard makers*]."

Wednesday, October 27th:

"The Mam went up to St Ann's to see the Thomases [*Rev. David Walter Thomas, M.A., was vicar of St Ann's, Bethesda until he became vicar of Holyhead in 1895*] and had a very pleasant day. Georgie went to college. Mollie had visitors and put away dresses."

Thursday, October 28th:

"Heard from Treiorwerth this morning: the Archdeacon is better but has sent in his resignation of the archdeaconary to the Bishop. [*Rev. J. Wynne-Jones was succeeded as Archdeacon of Bangor by Grace Vincent's friend, Canon John Pryce.*] Hugh and Gustie out ferreting all afternoon but had a very poor day. Heard a very bad account of poor Jim [*Johnson*], Mollie has offered to go to Llaniestyn."

Friday, October 29th:

"Mollie went off to Llaniestyn by the 4.10 train. Georgie drove with her to Bangor, she had a rush for the train."

Saturday, October 30th:

"The Mam and Georgie alone at home. The boys [*Hugh and Gustie*] went off at 7 o'clock to play in a football match for Carnarvon at Stoke and did not return until 2 a.m.. The Mam waited up for them. They had had a good game but been badly beaten and were very tired. They had been to a theatre in Chester on their way back." [*At the beginning of the 1886-7 season Carnarvon Wanderers had become the first North Wales team to enter the English F.A. Cup competition. Hugh played half-back and was team captain. In this first round match they were completely outclassed by a professional team that included the England goalkeeper. To add to their woes, their own goalkeeper broke his wrist, making a save early in the match. The final score was 10-1. Legend has it that the Wanderers' share of the gate money was not enough to cover their return fare and the club secretary had to pawn his watch to get them home. The Vincent boys must have held on to their money so that they could console themselves with an evening out in Chester.*]

Sunday, October 31st:

"Letters from Mollie Ted, Lil, Will and Eva. Eva and Will are coming home on Friday [*having been in Ireland since October 11th*]. Went to the Cathedral. Gustie brought home a friend to dinner. Both the boys are very tired, Hugh asleep on the sofa snoring horribly. Weather: west wind and sun."

Monday, November 1st:

"The boat carried up for the winter and put in the barn."

Tuesday, November 2nd:

"Hugh had 12 cases at the Carnarvon County Court, out of which he won 11."

Wednesday, November 3rd:

"Very wet day. Played whist in the evening."

Thursday, November 4th:

"Lil and Jack's little girl born [*Evangeline Sarah Grace, known as Grace*]. The Mam busy packing to go off to her tomorrow. Hugh playing football. Gustie came out second in an English exam. Went to a dinner party at Treborth Hall to represent the family as the Mam and Hugh were unable to go."

Friday, November 5th:

"Mother went off to Lil. Mollie came back from Llaniestyn. Dora Ramsay came with her from Afonwen and stayed the night here. It rained all day. Georgie's cold not better. Mollie was up a good deal in the night watching for Eva and Will who were coming home. Some mistake was made about the train so they did not arrive until half past five in the morning. Harry Griffith came with them. [*Harry was now a medical student at Trinity College, Dublin.*] Gustie wasn't well, over-tired. Mollie had tea at Hugh's office, very good. She found a Wedgewood dish there and brought it home. Mollie bought Froude's new book *Oceana* on her way home [*Oceana, or England and Her Colonies, published in 1886 by James Anthony Froude, subsequently Regius Professor of Modern History at Oxford*]."

Saturday, November 6th:

"Windy, cold, wet day. The boys could not run with the hounds as they intended, everyone was tired. Mr B. Griffith appeared at luncheon time and stayed. Harry went back to Pentraeth. Will walked past Treffos with him. Had a telegram from Mother to say she had got to her journey's end and that Lil and the baby were both well. Bought the smoking room lamp and a fresh gallon of oil. Sent pears to Jim [*Johnson*]."

Sunday, November 7th:

"We went to the Cathedral, heard a sermon on Church Defence from Mr Thomson Jones. Quartet out of *Elijah*, 'O Everyone that Thirsteth'. The Cathedral was rather badly decorated for 'Harvest Home'."

Monday, November 8th:

"Annie Williams [*the niece of Lady Louisa Ramsay*] came to luncheon on her way to the Hunt. Frank Watkin-Davies also appeared unexpected but delightful as usual. Mary Sackville-West rode over and sat in a very wet habit and had tea in Georgie's room. Mary Davies came afterwards and was very nice as usual. Miserable day."

Tuesday, November 9th:

"Wet day. Hugh went to the hunt with the Sackville-Wests and stayed. Mary Davies sent Georgie some beautiful chrysanthemums."

Wednesday, November 10th:

"Eva and Mollie went and had luncheon at Treborth Hall to meet Miss Wyatt. Looked through all Mary's and her sketches. They were nice especially Mary's. Miss Wyatt coming in to dinner."

[*The next entries are made by Mother, Grace Elizabeth Vincent.*]

Wednesday, November 17th:

"Evangeline Margaret Vincent died suddenly."

Saturday, November 20th:

"Buried at Llanbeblig in her father's grave. Present: her mother, Mollie, Georgie, Edmund, Hugh, Will and Gustie; Canon Johnson, John Lloyd-Williams [*Jack*], Hugh Johnson, David Bankes-Price, the Hon. Mrs Wynne-Jones, Grace Parry, Mary and Trixie Davies."

There follows a list, in Mollie Vincent's handwriting, of 143 people who sent letters of tribute and condolence to the family, and Elizabeth Barrett Browning's poem 'The Sleep', copied by Ted Vincent.

Of all the thoughts of God that are
Borne inward into souls afar,
     Along the Psalmist's music deep,
Now tell if that any is
For gifts or grace surpassing this –
     "He giveth His beloved sleep."

What would we give to our beloved?
The hero's heart to be unmoved,
     The poet's star-tuned harp to sweep,
The patriot's voice to teach and rouse,
The monarch's crown to light the brows?
     He giveth His beloved sleep.

What do we give to our beloved?
A little faith in all undisproved,
     A little dust to over weep,
And bitter memories to make
The whole world blasted for our sake.
     He giveth His beloved sleep.

"Sleep soft beloved!" we sometimes say
Who have no time to charm away
     Sad dreams that through the eyelids creep.
But never doleful dream again
Shall break the happy slumber, when
     He giveth His beloved sleep.

O Earth, so full of dreary noises!
O men, with wailing in your voices!
     O delved gold, the wailer's heap!
O strife, O curse, that o'er it fall
God strikes a silence through you all,
     And giveth His beloved sleep.

His dews drop mutely o'er the hill,
His cloud above it raileth still,
        Though on its slope men sow and reap.
More softly than the dew is shed
Or cloud is floated overhead
        He giveth His beloved sleep.

Ay! Men may wonder while they scan
A living, thinking, feeling man
        Confirmed in such a rest to keep;
But angels say, and through the word
I think their happy smile is heard,
        "He giveth His beloved sleep."

For me, my heart that erst did go
Most like a tired child at show
        That sees through tears the mummers leap,
Would now its wearied vision close,
Would child-like on his love repose –
        He giveth His beloved sleep.

And friends, dear friends, when it shall be
That this low breath is gone from me
        And round my bier ye come to weep;
Let one most loving of you all
Say, "Not a tear must o'er her fall."
        He giveth His beloved sleep.

The Diary contains no further entries.

Part Five : What the Future Held

9. THE LIVES and ACHIEVEMENTS of the VINCENTS of TREBORTH

The Family Diary begins on New Year's Day 1885 recording Evangeline Vincent having to go to bed, unwell; it ends abruptly with her death in November 1886, eight days after her twenty-third birthday. There are many references to Eva suffering bouts of poor health, but she always recovers and her death seems to have come as a great shock to the family. On the first occasion the family sent for Dr Prydderch of Menai Bridge and it was he who signed her death certificate, giving the cause of death as anaemia. She was buried alongside her late father in Llanbeblig churchyard. The very private funeral service was conducted by her cousin Will Wynne-Jones. He would perform this service many times for the Vincents.

Grace Elizabeth Vincent
(1828-1899)

Grace Vincent lived to see all her surviving children but Mollie and Augustus, married. She was a grandmother many times over by the time she died at the age of 70, in January 1899. Prayers were said at Treborth Uchaf before the funeral, led by John Pryce, who was now the Archdeacon of Bangor. He was related to Grace by marriage, was Ted's godfather and had been a friend of the family for well over 40 years. She was buried alongside her husband and daughter by Will Wynne-Jones. Grace's obituary in the *North Wales Chronicle* spoke of her as a woman "of acute intelligence and wide reading … remarkable energy and independence of spirit".

Mollie, the eldest daughter and chief keeper of the Family Diary, the owner of Treborth Uchaf and its estate, never married, but cared for her mother until her death, and then remained at Treborth Uchaf for the rest of her long life. There had been opportunities for marriage. The only surviving evidence for her engagement to Edward Cook, Ted's Winchester and Oxford friend and future brother-in-law, is to be found in a biography of Cook.[8] The author states that in the summer of 1880, after taking a First in Greats, Cook "announced with his usual sang-froid, from a weirdly-named house near Bangor, that he had become engaged to Miss Mary Vincent … This match was broken off." The book was written after Cook's death, but as it acknowledges the help of his family, specifically including Babs Vincent, it must be assumed to be factually accurate.

This relationship is not the only mystery attached to Mollie's private life. Mollie's niece, Lady Dorothy Arthur, told her family that her aunt, in old age, had confided to her that, "my temper cost me my engagement to Lionel Sackville-West". This does not seem a very likely match. Mollie was eight years older than Lionel, of plain appearance and modest income; she always described herself on census returns as a 'farmer'. Lionel, however, was the eldest nephew of Mortimer, first Lord Sackville, and third in line, after an uncle and his own father, to inherit Knole, the vast ancestral home near Sevenoaks in Kent, that required a staff of 60 to run it, and was one of the great treasure houses of England.

There is also the problem of when such an engagement and break-up could have taken place. In the Family Diary it is clear that he is nothing more to her than the younger brother of her friends Mary and Cecilie. He is a teenager who runs and hunts with her own younger brother, Will, and still has years of education to complete. By the end of the Diary in 1886, Lionel is a history undergraduate at

---

[8] J. Saxon Mills, *Sir Edward Cook K.B.E.*, London, Constable & Co., 1921.

Oxford. It is possible, of course, that the nature of their relationship could have changed during a university vacation, but is it probable that Mollie would have embarked upon what, for the time would have been a rather whirlwind romance, so soon after the trauma of her sister's death, or that Lionel, enjoying life as a student, would have been thinking of marriage? At about the time he was finishing his studies, his fancy was taken elsewhere. In 1888 Mortimer died and Knole passed to his next brother, who was also called Lionel. He returned to Britain from Washington, where he had been head of the British legation, to take up his inheritance, bringing with him his vivacious and beautiful illegitimate daughter, Victoria. In June 1890, Lionel Sackville-West married his cousin. Although ultimately not successful, the marriage was by all accounts a love-match. He had to overcome opposition from everyone in his family except his uncle, the bride's father. One argument was that her four-year seniority was too great an age gap – how much more they would have objected to Mollie!

There is, however, the possibility that the young man in Mollie's life has been misidentified; that she spoke with regret about 'Lionel' and the wrong inference was drawn because of the known friendship between the Vincents and Sackville-Wests. This is supported by evidence that there was indeed another, more mysterious Lionel in her life.

In 1882 Mollie attempted to keep a private diary; it is sporadic and – for a family historian – frustratingly enigmatic. During the year she made several visits to Dublin to see her brother Hugh at Trinity College, staying with relatives outside the city. On one occasion she described herself as very cross because surprise visitors prevented her from going into Dublin, and while she is never explicit, it is clear from the sub-text of her entries that the main attraction is her brother's friend, Lionel. All the other young men she meets in Hugh's rooms are recorded by their surnames; some of them appear years later in the Diary and are still described with polite formality. Lionel, on the other hand, is never given a surname. A search of Trinity College registers reveals no student with this Christian name at this time. Perhaps he was a connection through their Irish relatives rather than the college. Whoever he was, there is an undeniable coyness when, after watching Hugh and Lionel play cricket, she says, "a certain person looked A1 in his cricket whites". She also describes her twenty-third birthday, spent in the company of Hugh and Lionel, as her "best ever".

Lionel came to Treborth Uchaf to spend both Easter and Christmas 1882 with the Vincents. He also visited in July but Mollie seems to have enjoyed herself too much to bother about her diary: "July 26th, Lionel came and we had a jolly day, ditto 27th,28th,29th, 30th, 31st. Lionel went away that night." That summer she played tennis with the new racket he had sent her as a present. There is a brief mention of him in August, "Troops being sent out to Egypt daily. Lionel at Hythe pro tem." The juxtaposition of these two sentences suggests that Lionel is in the army; there was a musketry school in the town and Shorncliffe military camp was just outside.

Mollie seems to have lost all interest in her diary by the end of the year and the tone becomes noticeably downbeat. Both November and December are given jumbled, retrospective entries and a two-day visit by Lionel in November is only mentioned at the end of the year. The obvious time for a young family friend to come in November would have been the week of the hunt balls in Beaumaris. In the middle of her account of this highlight of the local social calendar, there is an intriguing sentence that bears no relation to what comes before or after: "So much for September 4th 1879 on which the 'golden days' began, they ended November 9th 1882, and I don't regret them for themselves, only am sorry they are over, for lots of reasons." Was this the end of her friendship with Lionel? No mention was made of an engagement but had they come to an understanding? If so, it must have been awkward when, presumably already invited as Hugh's friend, he came for Christmas. Mollie merely stated, "Lionel was here". If speculation about this mysterious entry is correct, it means she got engaged to Cook after meeting Lionel, but many plausible explanations could be offered for this.

The Lionel mentioned in the Family Diary is always explicitly or implicitly Lionel Sackville-West, with the exception of the entry for September 20th 1886, when the Lionel with whom Hugh is spending some time in London is perhaps more likely to be his old Dublin friend than the teenager from Bangor.

The truth is probably lost, but however many broken engagements, and however many Lionels there were in Mollie Vincent's life, it is certain that she suffered emotional disappointment. She dedicated her life to local charities and the Church. For a period around the time of the First World War, she ran a small school at her home for the children of the villagers of Treborth. Mollie was a well known figure in Bangor and had a wide circle of friends, both locally and further afield. She travelled widely, and often visited cathedrals in Britain and on the continent, returning with additions to her scrap books and photograph albums. On one occasion, in company with her friend Mary Davies of Treborth Hall, she spent several months in India. She was extremely fond of animals of all kinds, and is

MollieVincent (1859-1952) in the garden of Treborth Uchaf, with her brother, William, in the uniform of High Sheriff of Anglesey, 1931.

reputed to have shared her home at one period, with no fewer than 64 cats, many of these with various handicaps and missing parts. Mollie was the last survivor but one of the Vincent siblings. She died in October 1952, at the fine age of 93, and joined other members of her family in Llanbeblig churchyard.

Mollie lived on her own at Treborth Uchaf for a few years after her mother's death, until she was rejoined by her youngest brother, Augustus. After passing his army entrance examinations in 1886, Gustie Vincent continued his studies at the University College in Bangor for several terms before being commissioned into the 1st Battalion of the Royal Warwickshire Regiment. He specialised in ballistics and was, for two years, musketry instructor to the 3rd and 4th Battalions of the regiment. He served in the Boer War, commanding a machine-gun detachment at the Battle of Colenso and in the following campaign that culminated in the relief of Ladysmith in February 1900. Gustie was, reportedly, one of the first to enter the town after it had been besieged by the Boers for four months. He came away from the Boer War with the South Africa medal and three bars for his bravery, and a wound in the spine that seems to have ended his career as a soldier. He stayed on in South Africa as a member of the Natal Mounted Police, but returned home debilitated by his wounds, and would appear never again to have enjoyed full health. By all accounts, however, he was blessed with a very cheerful disposition that made him many friends, to whom he was universally known as 'Uncle Gus'.

He maintained his interest in Bangor Football Club for which he had been a leading player as a boy and took up golf with enthusiasm. He was, not surprisingly, a splendid shot and this was a pastime he shared with his close friend Lloyd Davies of Treborth Hall. In 1913 Lloyd Davies was killed in a mysterious shooting accident, close to the lake on the Treborth Hall estate. It was a blow, Mollie believed, from which Gustie never recovered.

On the outbreak of war in August 1914, Gustie volunteered to act as a recruiting officer for North Wales and the Marches. He was engaged in this work at meetings in Bangor and Bethesda on the evening of September 5th, but came home feeling unwell. The following day pneumonia was diagnosed and he underwent an emergency operation, but died the next morning. He had just celebrated his forty-sixth birthday. His funeral took the form of a service at Treborth Uchaf, led by the Dean of Bangor, followed by interment in the family grave, conducted by Will Wynne-Jones. Mollie must have felt the loss keenly. "He was," she wrote in one of her notebooks, "the most popular member of the family."

The eldest of the generation, Edmund Vincent was less than two years older than Mollie, and despite the fact that his education took him away from home at a very early age, his letters to her at various stages of their lives suggest that they

James Edmund Vincent (1857-1909) M.A., LL.B., barrister, journalist and author.

155

were very close. In 1884 he had embarked upon a career at the Bar and marriage. By marrying Mary Cook ('Babs'), Ted entered a literary family. Babs herself was an accomplished writer who regularly contributed articles and essays to leading journals and reviews, and besides her journalist brother, Edward, she had other brothers who combined legal and literary careers. Ted quickly followed their example, practising as a barrister on the North-western and North Wales Circuit and reporting for the *Law Times*.

In 1886 he became a special correspondent of *The Times*. His early articles, preserved by a proud Mollie, were mostly about country pursuits such as shooting and fishing. The same year, he used his knowledge and love of football (he had played for Oxford against Cambridge) to produce, in collaboration with another barrister, *A History of Football* – the first-ever book on the subject. As recorded in the Diary, 1886 was also the year his first child, Violet Mary, was born. His family was completed by the arrival of another daughter, Margaret Crawley, in 1893. They first lived in Fulham, and moved during the 1890s to Chelsea.

In 1890 he was appointed Chancellor of the Diocese of Bangor, a position that required legal qualifications. He wrote to his brother Gustie, telling him that he would not need to come home as there was no installation ceremony, he simply had to subscribe to the 39 Articles and the Queen's supremacy. He drew a sketch of the personal seal that came with the post, joking that what looked like tadpoles and fowl were actually fish and eagles. Despite his flippancy, it was a position he took very seriously and held for the rest of his life. Like his brother Hugh, Ted was a staunch supporter of Anglican establishment and a defender of the Church's endowments in Wales.

The Times quickly asked him to report more widely on sport, but trying to build two careers simultaneously must have caused him occasional difficulties. Mollie kept one of his letters which was obviously written in reply to her concerns about how he could spend a fortnight covering Wimbledon, when he had a case due to come up in Caernarfon. He says that if the case is called, he will travel up on the overnight train and return to Wimbledon in the evening, confident that correspondents on rival papers will share enough information on the day's play for him to file his report. More practically, he says, he cannot afford to give up the £80 *The Times* had offered him for two weeks' work.

In 1894 Ted became the editor of the *National Observer* and held the post for three years, before becoming one of the founding editors of *Country Life* magazine in 1897. His connection with *The Times* continued, and he was made their specialist on industrial disputes in a period that saw many major strikes and lock-outs. He also became the paper's principal descriptive reporter for the more important public functions round the country, both political and royal.

It was Ted who wrote *The Times* account of the death of Queen Victoria. Reporting such a momentous event, the death of the only monarch that he and the majority of his fellow Britons had ever known, should have been a landmark in his career, but it was not without embarrassment for him. The nation's press, including Ted, descended on the Isle of Wight in January 1901, having been notified that the Queen was dying at Osborne, her home on the island. They gathered at the gate for four cold days, but when the announcement came on the evening of January 23rd, Ted Vincent, representing the most famous newspaper in the world, was not there. He defended himself at the end of his report, which appeared the following day, by saying that he had absented himself, knowing that the news would be telegraphed to London for proclamation by the Lord Mayor, before being given to the journalists at the gate. He was correct but, nevertheless, Ted admitted that he was shocked when, as he drove towards Osborne, he was passed in the opposite direction by "a crowd of carriages at the gallop, of bicycles careering down the hill at breakneck speed, of runners bawling 'Queen dead' at the top of their voices".

This lapse, if such it was, does not seem to have been held against him by his editor, who soon afterwards sent him to accompany the new heir to the throne, the future George V, on his tour of Australia, New Zealand, South Africa and Canada. Here, however, he did incur his employers' displeasure by submitting a large expenses claim that included 102 new shirts for a tour that lasted 210 days.

His next post as part-time motoring correspondent could be seen as a demotion, but it gave him time to write more books. It was also at about this time that he moved his family out of London to Drayton, Berkshire, where he was able to pursue his love of country sports and indulge in a passion he shared with many other Vincents, gardening. In all, Ted wrote 13 books, including an authorised biography of the Duke of Clarence, the two-volume *Land Tenancy in Wales*, and *The History of the Thames,* the manuscript of which he had just finished when he was suddenly taken ill in 1909. Pleurisy was diagnosed and he was taken to a London nursing home, where he died on July 18th, at the age of 52.

The Times obituary was warm, saying "a genial nature and cheery disposition made for him a host of friends," and "he had a great facility, a bright and distinctive style and the knack of imparting to his accounts … the touch that reveals a man of education and shrewd judgement … Mr Vincent had the gift of making people both like and trust

Ted Vincent (in the front passenger seat) in his role as motoring correspondent of *The Times.*

him and this was often of great value to him and the newspaper which he served." In response, there appeared in the letters page an additional tribute to "the loyalty of his friendship and the graceful and generous way in which he remembered and acknowledged even quite trivial assistance … If he could do a friend a good turn, he would never miss the chance."

He was buried at Brookwood, near Bisley, in Surrey with his cousin Will Wynne-Jones officiating. A friend, the Reverend Llewelyn R. Hughes, Rector of Llandudno, wrote a letter to *The Times* advocating a memorial and a fund was set up. Subscriptions were limited to five shillings (25p) but the money for a brass tablet was quickly raised. This memorial with its Latin inscription was unveiled and dedicated by Will Wynne-Jones at a special service in December 1910. It is mounted on the south wall of Bangor Cathedral, next to the plaque to the memory of his grandfather, Dean Vincent.

The second daughter of the family was Ellen Augusta Crawley Vincent, who seems to have been known by all, throughout her life, as 'Lil'. She was, by all accounts, a remarkable woman, who touched the hearts and lives of many people. Her marriage in the first year of the Family Diary took her to Cardiganshire, to Lampeter College and its school where her husband, John Jordan (Jack) Lloyd-Williams, was headmaster. They moved to Carmarthen in 1887 and to Oswestry in 1892 where Jack was successively and very successfully headmaster of the towns' grammar schools.

In the seventeen years between 1886 and 1903, Lil bore eleven children, nine daughters and two sons. In 1909 the family moved again so that Jack could take up the headship of Ruthin School but three years later his health broke down. At the age of just 53, he was forced to retire to Brynele, the home in Cardiganshire that he and Lil had built, but with more than half their children still at various stages of their education, they could not afford for her to join him. Having always closely supported her husband in his career, Lil had had plenty of opportunities to observe teaching and school organization; armed with this knowledge and the managerial skills that accrue with bringing up a large family, she set about founding her own school. In 1913 she opened a school for girls in Lloran House, a large town house in Oswestry, since demolished. It was a modest beginning with just eleven pupils: her own three younger daughters, four nieces and the daughters of friends. Lil's two elder daughters, Grace, a linguist, and Mary, a musician, came to help their mother teach. The headmaster of Oswestry Boys' Grammar School gave science lessons and other tutors were brought in as occasion demanded. Even the family cook added her talents to the venture.

The modest beginning of Lloran House School: the headmistress 'Aunt Lil' is flanked by her two eldest daughters, Grace and Mary, and surrounded by her pupils.

Jack would come to see his wife and her school, giving the girls some classical education, and it was at Lloran House that he died in 1916. Lil did not allow her grief to dilute her energies, however, and the school became so successful that in 1919, in order to expand, she purchased Moreton Hall and its estate at Weston Rhyn, just on the English side of the Welsh border. The school went from strength to strength, and flourishes to the present day. Remarkably, Lil continued as headmistress, despite suffering from Parkinson's disease, until her death, just two weeks before her eightieth birthday. Throughout this period she was supported by her brothers and sisters. Hugh and Georgie sent their daughters to Lloran House, and later generations of Ted's family went to Moreton Hall. In the very early days, it was Mollie who presented the school with a proper uniform from a London designer. Hugh was a regular visitor and so, later, was William. She started by teaching her nieces but to generations of girls, often drawn from the same families, she was affectionately known and remembered as 'Aunt Lil'.

She was buried alongside her husband in the churchyard at Trefilan, between Lampeter and Aberaeron in central Wales. The newspaper obituaries were effusive. *The Times* said, "Mrs Lloyd-Williams was the centre of a world for all lovers of the cultural side of life – music, art, literature and drama – in the district and far beyond, and the thousands of letters received from Old Boys of her husband's schools and from Old Moretonians show the deep love and esteem which were inspired by her wonderful personality. She radiated humour, charm and kindliness, allied to that intellectual ability which made her an unforgettable headmistress." The *North Wales Chronicle* declared, "There was nothing small or narrow in her nature. She lived for others, not sparing herself – her common sense, apt criticisms, and humour made her a delightful companion." Agreeable though these are, Lil might have preferred as an epitaph the comments made during her life-time by an Archbishop of Wales who said, "her wit and common-sense are worth a whole benchful of bishops," and that, "she lives in the sunshine of her soul."

Lil had another memorial in the success of her children. Both of her sons were awarded the Military Cross in the First World War, and both subsequently became chief constables, the elder for Worcestershire and the younger for Cardiganshire; but more remarkable for their generation was the level of education and achievement of her nine daughters. Eight of the girls were given a university or college education. The ninth, who chose to go into specialised nursing, later

Ellen Lloyd-Williams (1860-1940) with her grandson on her lap (second right), and her eleven children and in-laws at the wedding of her daughter Elizabeth. They are on the front lawn of Moreton Hall School.

went on to become matron successively at Shrewsbury, Harrow and Eton schools. Five daughters graduated from the University of London and two from the Royal Academy of Music. Another, Sylvia, read sciences at Girton College, Cambridge, and was a senior house-mistress at Roedean before becoming headmistress at King Edward VI's School for Girls in Birmingham. One of the London graduates, Kitty, proceeded from Bedford College, London, to the Royal Free Hospital, where she took her M.D. degree and gained a Fellowship of the Royal College of Surgeons. She was the first woman to be made Dean and Medical Superintendent of the Royal Free Hospital, and went on to be Dean of the Faculty of Medicine in the University of London. In recognition of her achievements she was appointed a Commander of the British Empire. Another daughter, named Ellen Augusta after her mother, was a linguist who wrote and spoke six languages, and entered the diplomatic service. Grace and Mary, the two daughters who had helped their mother start her school, succeeded her as joint headmistresses and on Mary's death in 1945, their sister Bronwen gave up a journalistic career in London and became headmistress, a post she held until 1972.

The Vincent who forged a career in his home town was Hugh. Following an arts degree at Trinity College, Dublin, he read for his law examinations in London chambers and had just commenced practising as a solicitor during the period of the Family Diary. He went on to build up a large and very successful practice, Carter, Vincent & Co., with offices in Caernarfon and Bangor. The company became solicitors to the Penrhyn estate and always represented the Penrhyn family in legal matters, notably in the case arising from the great three-year Penrhyn quarry strike of 1900 to 1903, which was a landmark in the history of the British trade union movement. He was appointed clerk to the Bangor magistrates in 1906 and held the post for 25 years. His business interests included ownership of the Cilgwyn slate quarries in the Vale of Nantlle, and he was a director of both the Alliance Assurance Company and the *North Wales Chronicle*. He would seem to have been an enlightened employer: he guaranteed employment upon their return home to all quarrymen at Cilgwyn who joined the services in the First World War, a far from universal practice at the time.

Hugh had got married in 1892 to Bronwen Adelaide Trevor, the daughter of a well known Welsh Churchman, and together they raised a family of five daughters and one son. Their first home was a semi-detached house in Upper Bangor and then they built a large house, Bronwydd, on the Treborth Uchaf estate, adjacent to the old family home. The young man's sports of football and rugby gave way to golf, and his photograph still hangs in the entrance of the Bangor Golf Club, where he was captain from 1916 to 1920. His love of tennis seems to have been life-long: he created a grass court at Bronwydd, and at the holiday home he bought in 1919 in Trearddur Bay, there remains a flat area the size of a tennis court cut into a sloping lawn.

There could have been very little time, however, in his life for recreation, so many were the public duties that he undertook. He was a member of Bangor City Council for fifteen years, and was unanimously elected mayor in 1908. He held the post for three consecutive years but declined when offered a fourth term on account of business responsibilities. The high-point of his period of office was welcoming the new king, George V, when he came to Bangor in 1911, to open the Pritchard Jones Hall at the University College. During the same year , Hugh also sat on the committee that made the local arrangements for the investiture of the Prince of Wales. At other times he sat on the county council and was a governor of the College. He was for many years president of the Carnarvon Boroughs Unionist Association and president of the Bangor Conservative Association.

Sir Hugh Vincent (1862-1931) solicitor. He served as Mayor of Bangor for three consecutive years from 1908 to 1911.

He was a staunch Conservative, a tireless worker for the party, and a politician of conviction. It was the strength of his beliefs that led him to step, briefly, into the national spotlight. In 1909 the House of Lords rejected the Liberal government's Budget, an action without precedent in 250 years. The powers of the Lords and the fate of "the People's Budget" became major political issues. The central figure in the political and constitutional struggle was the Chancellor of the Exchequer who had proposed the budget: David Lloyd George, M.P. for Carnarvon Boroughs. When the widely expected election was finally called by Prime Minister Asquith, at the end of the year, the local Conservative party did not have a candidate. Lloyd George had taken the seat from the Conservatives in 1890 by the smallest of margins but over the intervening 20 years he had built a glittering career and had turned the constituency into a political and personal stronghold. Eminent local Conservatives, such as the Vincents' friend, Colonel Henry Platt of Llanfairfechan, had failed to make any impression on his majority. Whoever stood against him at this particular election would be subject to national publicity, which was how Hugh's photograph came to fill the front page of the *Daily Mirror* for December 14th 1909. If Hugh was reluctant to put his name forward, it was understandable. His reasons for doing so can be extrapolated from a speech he gave to the local Primrose League before his candidacy was announced. He denounced Liberal policies as attacks on the Constitution, the Empire and the

The Daily Mirror

THE MORNING JOURNAL WITH THE SECOND LARGEST NET SALE.

MR. H. C. VINCENT, WHO WILL OPPOSE MR. LLOYD-GEORGE IN THE CARNARVON BOROUGHS AT THE GENERAL ELECTION.

(Left) The front page of the *Daily Mirror* for December 14th 1909. Hugh Vincent and his children are standing outside Bronwydd, his home in Treborth.

(Below) The openly partisan *North Wales Chronicle* gives last-minute encouragement to the voters of Bangor to vote Conservative.

THE CHRONICLE, FRIDAY, JANUARY 21, 1910.

VINCENT SCORES WITH TARIFF REFORM.

HOGYN O'R DRE! PLAY UP, BANGOR

164

Church: everything that he believed in and was willing to fight for.

Hugh fought an energetic campaign, sometimes speaking to as many as three meetings in one evening. He seems to have been very popular in Bangor and garnered a great deal of support in Hirael and Glanadda, traditionally the maritime and railway areas of the city, blaming Liberal Free Trade policies for the unemployment that was being suffered and demanding tariff reform. "I was born and have lived in the Carnarvon Boroughs all my life," he declared in one speech, "and have never in all my experience seen such misery and distress throughout the whole of the boroughs as now, arising out of the amount of unemployment prevailing. I cannot pretend to indulge in the flights of my opponent's oratorical fancy, but it is an idle mockery to pretend to deal with the working man's want by setting up bureaux for labour. The only remedy for unemployment is employment and to start labour bureaux when there is no employment is like starting up a shop with nothing to sell in it."

In other parts of the constituency, however, he sometimes had to struggle to be heard. At a meeting in the Carnarvon Pavilion, he was supported by F.E. Smith, one of Lloyd George's chief antagonists in Parliament. Hugh was heckled, but the attempts to prevent Smith speaking became so rowdy and violent that they reached the national press. Lloyd George was quick to disassociate himself, sending a telegram to the *Liverpool Daily Post and Mercury* that stated, "I wish to say that I appeal to my friends to give a fair hearing to my opponent, Mr Vincent, and not to disrupt his meetings. I am all for free speech."

The violence on this occasion, however, was nothing to that which Caernarfon experienced on polling day, when an estimated 2,000 quarrymen descended on the town. Trouble had been anticipated and a large number of policeman from Manchester had been brought in, but because they were not sworn-in, they did not have the power to arrest and could only step in and attempt to break up the street fights that ensued. The windows of shops and public houses were smashed; people wearing Conservative colours were attacked; Will Wynne-Jones who, after 25 years as vicar, was probably the most popular man in the town, was kicked and punched; allegedly, even a five-year old girl had her jacket torn off and ripped apart because it was blue.

Behaviour at the count was more gentlemanly: Lloyd George polled 3,183 votes, Hugh Vincent received 2,105. Hugh had brought the Chancellor's majority down by 300, when the Liberal majority in neighbouring constituencies had increased. Magnanimous in victory, Lloyd George congratulated Hugh on his campaign and thanked him for the manner in which he had conducted it. Immediately after the election, Hugh told party workers that he would be happy to stand again, but before Britain could hold another general election, both the country and Hugh's life had changed irrevocably.

In August 1914, Britain declared war on Germany and the Austro-Hungarian Empire. Hugh's only son, James Trevor Crawley Vincent, was already a second lieutenant in the 2nd Battalion of the Welsh Regiment, but aged only 18, was not old enough to fight. He instructed recruits in Cardiff until January 1915, when he was allowed to go to the front. He was killed four months later on May 9th at St Vaast, France, while leading his platoon in an assault on enemy trenches. Five other young lieutenants were killed in the action. When the notification came, the agony for his parents must surely have been compounded by the news that, because the assault had been unsuccessful, his body was still lying on the battlefield. Mercifully, another letter came within days to say that his body had been recovered.

By all accounts, Hugh never fully recovered from the loss of his son. In the 1920s many British families went to the newly created war cemeteries in France and Belgium. Hugh and family made the sad pilgrimage in 1925. It was ten years after James' death, but the impact on Hugh is evident from the poignant letter he sent Mollie.

My dear Mol,

I am sorry I couldn't write before, but we have been rather hurried from pillar to post. We have seen Jim's grave. I am glad I have seen it – it is very beautiful, and calm, and restful. It is difficult to realize that he lies there, but I am glad to know exactly what it is like. He was killed quite close to where he lies – I think I know almost the exact spot, and I understand the position of things on that morning when he started out. I can't tell you any more about it now, excepting that I think I feel happier about it all. I am never going to talk about it again. I think I understand better now, though all very cloudily.

We came to Paris yesterday evening and are going to stay here for two or three days, and then come home. Jim lies surrounded by boys from his own regiment, who started out with him that morning. They are all together.

Bron is quite well, and so are the chicks. Somehow, I can't write any more – but you will understand. I am really much happier.

Your loving brother,

Hugh

Hugh and Bronwen had a memorial to their son, carved on a stone quarried from the Treborth Uchaf estate, mounted beside the other Vincent memorials in Bangor Cathedral. Beneath it hangs the wooden cross that stood over his original battlefield grave. The loss of James was not the only tragedy to hit Hugh's family: his daughter Lilian would have announced her engagement to Andrew Irvine had he and George Mallory returned from the 1924 Everest expedition. She never married.

Hugh Vincent was knighted in Baldwin's resignation honours list of 1924. The citation was for public and political services. By this time his public work was mostly confined to the institution that was at the very centre of his life, the Church. Over the years he held almost every post in the Church open to a layman. During and after the 1910 election, he fought passionately against the Liberal plans to disestablish the Welsh Church, speaking throughout Wales and England. When the battle was lost, he threw his energies into stabilising the finances of the new, disendowed Church in Wales. For 34 years he worked for the Charity for the Relief of Widows and Orphans of Clergymen in the Bangor Diocese. A former choirboy himself, he took a life-long interest in the cathedral choir, giving the boys a Christmas party every year for over 40 years.

Sir Hugh Vincent died unexpectedly on April 22nd 1931, just five days before his sixty-ninth birthday, when an attack of influenza turned into double pneumonia. A prominent citizen, his death was given a great deal of coverage in the local press. The reports all give a picture of a man of great integrity; always prepared to stand up and be counted, he had as many opponents as allies but the sincerity and honesty of his position were so apparent that he was respected by all. His funeral service was held in Bangor Cathedral, where his daughters later erected a carved wooden screen to the Lady Chapel in his memory. He is buried, not at Llanbeblig, but in St Mary's churchyard, Llanfairpwllgwyngyll, looking across the Menai Strait towards his home on the mainland at Treborth.

William Vincent, the third son and sixth child, was the family member who rose to international eminence. Having prepared in London for the extremely competitive Indian Civil Service examinations, in which he was placed very high on the list in 1885, William completed his subsequent ICS training at Trinity College, Dublin and then in London. He embarked for India, at the age of 21, in the autumn of 1887 and arrived in Calcutta in December of that year. He started his Indian career in the executive branch of the provincial government of Bengal, based in Dacca and eventually became a District Officer. In 1900 he transferred from the executive to the judicial branch of government in Bengal as a District and Sessional Court judge, before being promoted in 1906 to Judicial Commissioner for Chota Nagpur, the large central area of Bihar and Orissa. In 1909 he was further advanced to the then capital of India, when he was appointed as a judge of the Calcutta Supreme Court.

In 1911, in a career move which was unusual in the ICS, William Vincent returned to the executive branch when he was appointed to the Government of India by the new viceroy, Lord Hardinge. He also assumed the important role of Secretary of the Legislative Department of the Government of India, and this was followed by a knighthood in the New Year's honours list of 1913. A little over a year later, he was appointed to the three-man executive council of the government of Bihar and Orissa, a sideways step, which was seen as preparation for him to succeed to the governorship of the province. In the event, the emergency demands of the First World War led to Sir William's appointment as leader of the Mesopotamian Medical Commission in 1916. This was an inquiry into the failure of both the military and medical lines of supply which had led to disaster and heavy loss of life in the Indian Army's campaign in Mesopotamia. The unflinching and fearless honesty of the Vincent Report impressed both Indian and British governments alike. Another new viceroy, Lord Chelmsford, who took office in 1916, also wished to have Sir William at the centre of his government and recruited him to both the Council of India and the Viceroy's Executive Council.

Sir William Vincent became Home Member of the Government of India and President of the Viceroy's Council in April 1917. The office was second only to that of the Viceroy. Almost immediately, he produced an internal memorandum which contained proposals for the progression of India to self-government over a thirty-year period. India did indeed achieve full independence exactly 30 years later, in 1947, but not by the planned and measured stages he envisaged. As Home Member, Sir William was brought into the centre of the gathering troubles of the time. He was called upon to steer the unpopular national security legislation known as the Rowlatt Acts through the Legislature against almost unanimous Indian opposition. He was responsible for the maintenance of military recruitment as part of India's contribution to the final efforts of the First World War, and also the subsequent Afghan campaign. At the same time, he had to deal with much labour unrest and the first of Mohandas Gandhi's "non-violent" non-cooperation

Sir William Vincent (1866-1941) in an official photograph as Home Member of the Government of India, a position he held from 1917 to 1922.

movements. To add to all this, Sir William had to counter de-stabilising efforts to establish a popular boycott of the visit to India by the Prince of Wales.

When, in 1917, the new Secretary of State for India, Edwin Montagu, established a commission on Indian reform, Lord Chelmsford insisted that Sir William be a member. The Commission toured India in late 1917 and early 1918. In the latter year Sir William was appointed a Knight Commander of the Star of India. The Montagu Commission led to the 1919 India Act which established the new Legislative Assembly of the Government of India. Sir William Vincent was its first leader. He headed a government faced with an opposition in permanent majority; a position which required tact and the most delicate powers of persuasion.

Sir William's five years as Home Member must have been extremely stressful, and were not without danger. Amongst the papers he brought back to Britain is a letter containing a death threat. In one incident he narrowly avoided being kidnapped by Mahsud tribesmen when on a fact-finding mission; ten members of his convoy were seized and a driver killed. His next move was announced in 1922, but was not, as anticipated by many, to a provincial governorship. Instead, he was appointed to the Secretary of State's Council of India in London. When he left India in November 1922, Sir Willaim was further honoured as a Grand Commander of the Indian Empire. *The Times* recorded his 35 years of service in India under the heading, "Sir William Vincent: a Great Administrator". One Indian newspaper summed up his work by saying that, "At the back of all lay a deep love for India, a big capacity for hard work, a keen desire to give the country his best endeavour, and an abiding faith in the traditions of his service. Those were the essentials of the character of the Home Member who served through the most critical period of India's modern history."

Sir William returned to London and served as a member of the Secretary of State's Council of India from 1923 to 1931 under several Secretaries of State, including the Earl of Birkenhead, whose trenchant right-wing views on India must have caused him considerable disquiet. In 1925 he became Vice President of the Council of India and in 1926 was leader of the Indian delegation at the League of Nations in Geneva. To the end of his career, Sir William maintained a great number of close Indian friends both within and beyond government, and had the respect of a wide spectrum of Indian leaders, even those such as Gandhi, with whom he had at times clashed.

When he retired in 1931, Sir William returned to reside permanently at the family home with his sister Mollie in North Wales. He had married Grace Minna Trotter, the daughter of an Indo-Scottish family, only two years after arriving in India. This early marriage produced two daughters, Dorothy and Isabel, but appears to have been less than successful. There was certainly a degree of estrangement between William and his wife for a period of years prior to their return to Britain at the end of 1922, when they separated. Their elder daughter, Dorothy, remained in India with her husband Col. Sir Charles Gordon Arthur MC, who served with the Royal Field Artillery on the Western Front from 1915, and later commanded the Calcutta Light Horse. He was senior resident partner in Jardine Skinner & Co., East India Merchants, one of the great managing agency mercantile houses of British India in Calcutta. Charles Gordon Arthur became Sheriff of Calcutta, and was a civilian member of the Viceroy's Council. His and Dorothy's three children were Sir William's only grandchildren. The eldest, Allan James Vincent Arthur, was born in 1915 and given his two middle names in honour of Hugh's son, who had died earlier that year. He followed his grandfather into the Indian Civil Service and was Deputy Commissioner for Multan in the Punjab at the time of Independence in August 1947.

During the last ten years of his life, Sir William Vincent was frequently invited to speak on India to concerned parliamentary and university groups, and his speeches were widely reported by the press. This was the period when successive governments sought to define the path towards Indian self-government, and were anxious to have the thoughts of one who had done much to advocate and initiate the processes of reform.

Within North Wales, Sir William was High Sheriff of Anglesey in 1931-32 and found time to be chairman of the North Wales Society for the Blind, a charity in which his sister, Mollie, had long been active, and to serve as a member of the board of the local hospital, the Carnarvonshire and Anglesey Infirmary. He worked with great zeal for the University College of North Wales, of which he was Treasurer from 1932 to 1940. He was a Council member of the federal University of Wales, which awarded him the honorary degree of LL.D. in 1937. Soon after this he began to resign from charity work as his health began to fail. William Vincent died from pulmonary bronchitis on 17th April 1941, and was buried in the family grave in Llanbeblig.

William Vincent's younger sister, Grace Georgiana, 'Georgie', also spent many years in India. She married Charles Maitland Hudson, whose name appears alongside that of her brother in the ICS examination list for 1885. Theirs must have been a slow-burning romance or a long engagement, because they did not marry until 1896. A few days before the wedding, the bride's mother began the celebrations by giving a large tea party for the children of the nearby Vaynol School, where Georgie frequently helped with classes. The ceremony itself took place in Bangor Cathedral on a cold, wet day in October. Afterwards, the couple set sail for the very different climate of India, where Charles returned to his post in the Bombay district. They had three daughters and a son, Philip, who was head boy at Shrewsbury, and went on to win the MC while serving with the King's Shropshire Light Infantry in the First World War. The three daughters were sent back to Britain to be educated at their Aunt Lil's schools. The eldest, named Evangeline Margaret after her dead aunt, and like her, known as Eva, also married into the ICS. Her husband, Hely Richard Lynch-Blosse, became Secretary to the Viceroy, Lord Chelmsford, a post which would have brought him into frequent contact with his wife's uncle, Sir William Vincent, who was a member of Chelmsford's Executive Council.

Georgie, at least, was back in Britain at the outbreak of war in 1914, because she was able to attend Gustie's funeral. During the war she was heavily involved in voluntary care of the wounded, and long after the Armistice, she continued to work for servicemen who had lost limbs. She and her husband spent the inter-war years living in retirement in the Holland Park area of London. She was widowed in May 1940 and it was either then, or after Will's death the following year, that she returned to live with Mollie at Treborth. For another decade the eldest and the youngest of the Vincent sisters lived on in the family home. Georgie died in December 1952, just two months after Mollie. Earlier that year, on February 14th, when Georgie was in her eighty-fourth year and Mollie was in her ninety-third, the sisters had celebrated 74 years of the Vincents at Treborth Uchaf.

The Vincent family grave in Llanbeblig churchyard, Caernarfon.

Genealogical Appendices

Thomas Vincent, Rector of Llanfachraeth (1677 - 1738) m. Jane Anwyl, dtr of Maurice Anwyl of Parc (1678 - 1742)

Catherine Vincent (1716 - 1793) m. Rev. Owen Jones, First Canon of Bangor (1707 - 1795)

Capt. John Jones, Pant Howel, Llandegfan, 9th Regt of Foot (1753 - 1823) m (his first cousin) Jane Vincent, dtr Rev. James Vincent, Second Canon of Bangor (1751 - 1812)

James Vincent Vincent, Dean of Bangor 1862 – 76 (1792 - 1876) m. Margaret Matilda Crawley, dtr Capt John Crawley RN (1802 - 1867)

Rev. James Crawley Vincent, Vicar of Llanbeblig, Caernarfon (1827 - 1869) m Grace Elizabeth Johnson, dtr Rev. William Johnson, Rector of Llanfaethlu (1828 - 1899)

Edmund Vincent (1830 - 1865)

Augustus Vincent (1833 - 1859)

Corbet Vincent (1840 -72)

John Vincent (1825 - 1857)

James Edmund (1857 - 1909)

Mary (1859 -1952)

Ellen (1860 - 1940)

Hugh (1862 - 1931)

Evangeline (1864 - 1886)

William (1866 - 1941)

Grace Georgiana (1867 - 1952)

Augustus (1868 - 1914)

Appendix 1: The Vincent family from Thomas Vincent and Jane Anwyl (married 1714) to 1885

GRUFFYDD AP CYNAN, KING OF WALES 1079 - 1137
|
OWAIN GWYNEDD, PRINCE OF NORTH WALES
|
Rhodri, Lord of Anglesey, bur. Holyhead 1195
|
Tomos ap Rhodri
|
Cariadog ap Tomos
|
Gruffydd ap Cariadog
|
Dafydd ap Gruffydd
|
Howel ap Dafydd
|
Meredydd ap Howel, living 1352
|
Evan ap Meredydd
|
Meredydd ap Evan   Angharad, dtr Einion ap Ithel, hs. Rhiwaedog
|
John ap Meredydd, of Clenenney   Gwenhwyfer, dtr Goronwy ap Evan of Gwynfryn (m. 1484)
|
Morys ap John, of Rhiwaedog and Clenenney, living 1511   Angharad
|
Robert ap Morys of Parc, living 1544   Lowry, dtr. Lewis ap Ifan
|
Lewis Anwyl of Parc   Elizabeth, dtr. Morys ap Ifan
|
Elizabeth, dtr. + hs Edward Herbert   Willliam Lewis Anwyl of Parc, Sheriff of Caerns 1637
|
Evan Anwyl

Appendix 2: The line of descent from
Gruffydd ap Cyan, King of Wales (1079 – 1197)
to Jane Anwyl who married Thomas Vincent in 1714

Richard de la Wood, of Woodhall Cheshire
|
Jenkin de la Wood
|
Arnold de la Wood
|
John de la Wood
|
William de la Wood of Llangwyfan, Aberffraw, Inquisitor of Anglesey 1567

Meredydd ap Hwlkin Lloyd of Glynllifon, living 1400-1425
|
Robert ap Meredydd   Elin Bulkely of Beaumaris

Owain ap Meyrick, of Bodeon, Anglesey   Elin

Elin

Huw ap Morys ap Lewis   Jane Wood

William Pugh Lewis   Jane Anwyl, dtr Lewis Anwyl of Parc, Llanfrothen

Morris Williams of Hafodgaregog, Sheriff of Meirioneth 1665   Lowry, dtr Morris Prytherch

Catherine Williams

Maurice Anwyl, living 1695   Joanna Price, Lligwy, Machynlleth

Jane Anwyl (1678 - 1742)

Descent from William de Corbet of Caus Castle

Sir Robert Corbet, (1230-1300)   Matilda de Arundel (d 1309)

Sir Thomas Corbet, (1281-1310) of Moreton Corbet, Shropshire

Sir Robert Corbet, (1304-1375) fought at Crecy 1346

Sir Roger Corbet, (d. 1394)   Margaret de Erdington (d. 1395)

Sir Robert Corbet, (d. 1440)   Margaret Mallory

Sir Roger Corbet, (d. 1468)

Sir Richard Corbet, (1451-1493) fought for Lancaster at Bosworth

Sir Robert Corbet of Moreton Corbet (1477-1513)

Sir Roger Corbet (1500-1538)   Anne Windsor, (d. 1563)

Sir Andrew Corbet (1522-1578) Sheriff of Shropshire 1551

Sir Vincent Corbet (1555-1623)

Robert Corbet (d. 1644)

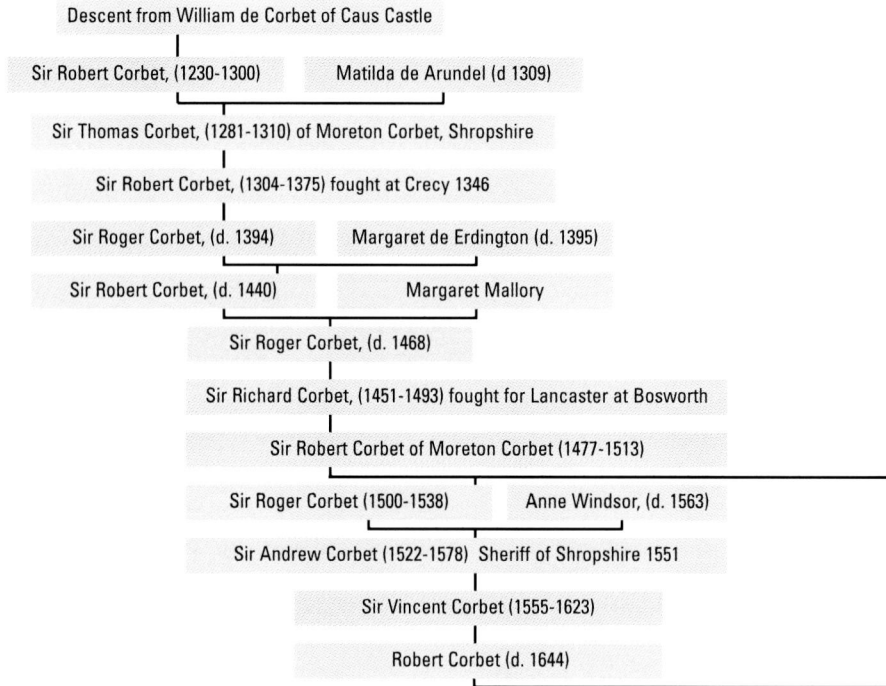

Appendix 3: The Vincent family descent through the
Corbets of Shropshire from
King Edward I of England (1239-1307)
to Thomas Vincent (1677-1738)

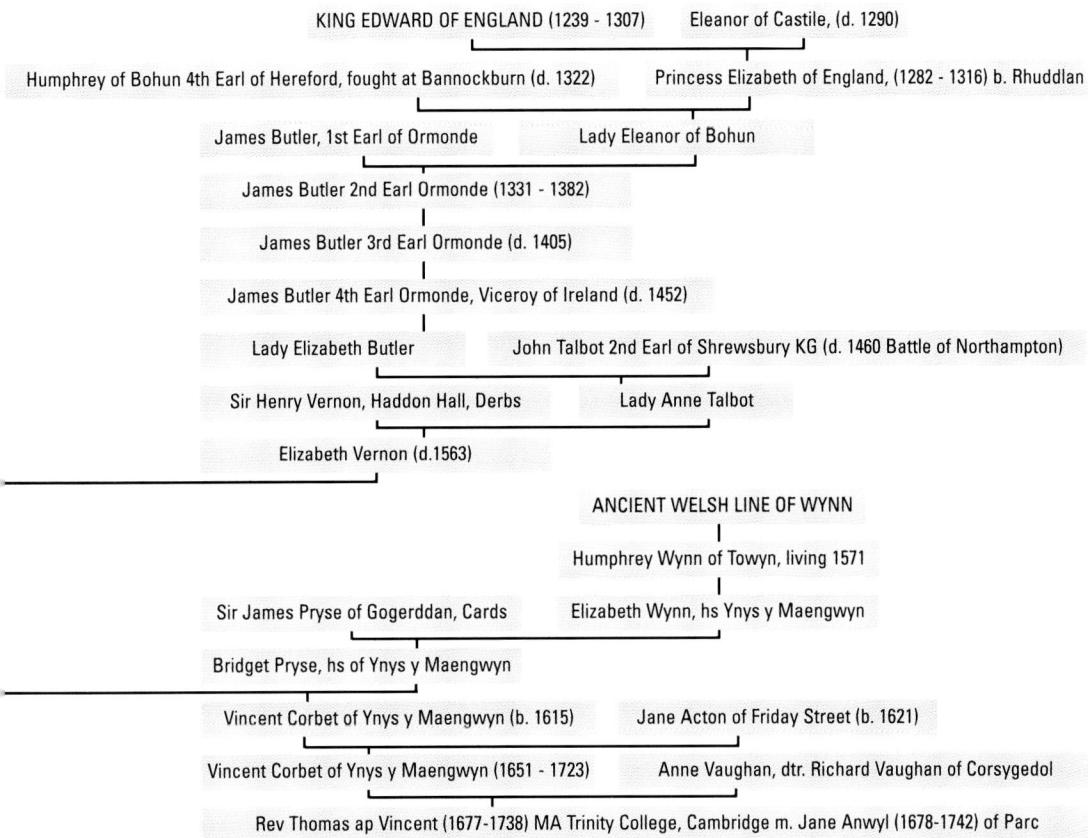

KING EDWARD OF ENGLAND (1239 - 1307)   Eleanor of Castile, (d. 1290)

Humphrey of Bohun 4th Earl of Hereford, fought at Bannockburn (d. 1322)   Princess Elizabeth of England, (1282 - 1316) b. Rhuddlan

James Butler, 1st Earl of Ormonde   Lady Eleanor of Bohun

James Butler 2nd Earl Ormonde (1331 - 1382)

James Butler 3rd Earl Ormonde (d. 1405)

James Butler 4th Earl Ormonde, Viceroy of Ireland (d. 1452)

Lady Elizabeth Butler   John Talbot 2nd Earl of Shrewsbury KG (d. 1460 Battle of Northampton)

Sir Henry Vernon, Haddon Hall, Derbs   Lady Anne Talbot

Elizabeth Vernon (d.1563)

ANCIENT WELSH LINE OF WYNN

Humphrey Wynn of Towyn, living 1571

Sir James Pryse of Gogerddan, Cards   Elizabeth Wynn, hs Ynys y Maengwyn

Bridget Pryse, hs of Ynys y Maengwyn

Vincent Corbet of Ynys y Maengwyn (b. 1615)   Jane Acton of Friday Street (b. 1621)

Vincent Corbet of Ynys y Maengwyn (1651 - 1723)   Anne Vaughan, dtr. Richard Vaughan of Corsygedol

Rev Thomas ap Vincent (1677-1738) MA Trinity College, Cambridge m. Jane Anwyl (1678-1742) of Parc

JOHN CRAWLEY of Nether Crawley c 1550: Lord of the Manor of Havering and of Luton, Beds

Thomas Crawley
m. Dorothy Edgerby of Milton, Oxon

Sir Frances Crawley Kt, DCL, Judge of the Court of Common Pleas
m. Elizabeth Rotheram

Sir Frances Crawley of Northaw Herts (d.1683) called to the Bar 1655
m. Mary Clutterbuck

Richard Crawley
m. Sarah Dashwood

Edmund Crawley of Halifax and Pictou Nova Scotia. HM Council for Nova Scotia
m. Matilda Randall

Admiral Edward Crawley RN (d.1834)
m. Elizabeth Jones b. 1758 of Castellmai, Caernarfon

Mary Matilda Crawley (b. 1788) Inherited Treborth Uchaf from her mother and bequeathed it to her brother

Ven. Edmund Jones Crawley Prebendary of Wells (b. 1792) Inherited Treborth Uchaf and bequeathed it to the Vincents

Appendix 4: The Vincent family descent from
John Crawley (c.1550) to
James Crawley Vincent (1827-1869) who
married Grace Elizabeth Johnson in 1855

Captain John Crawley RN (d. 1815) of Gorddinog, Llanfairfechan
m. Margaret Roberts (1778-1843) of Aber Rectory, nr Bangor

Margaret Matilda Crawley (1802-67)
m. James V. Vincent, Dean of Bangor (1792-1876)

Rev. James Crawley Vincent (1827-69)
m. Grace Elizabeth Johnson (1828-99)

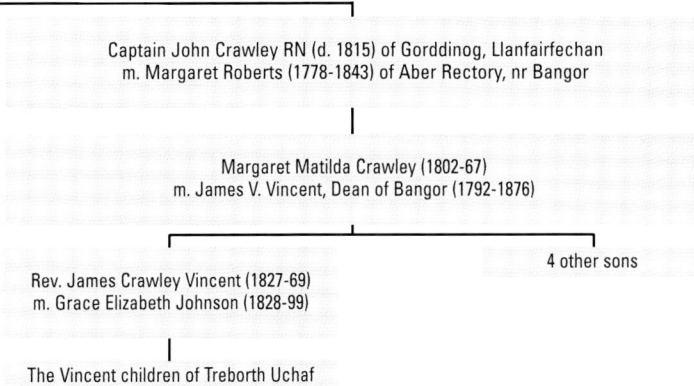

4 other sons

The Vincent children of Treborth Uchaf

Rev. Hugh Wynne-Jones, Prebendary of Penmynydd (1751-1809)
m. Grace Williams , dtr Rev. Robert Williams Rector Llanystumdwy (1754-1816)

Rev. Hugh Wynne-Jones, Rector of Llantrisant, Chancellor of Bangor (1776-1849)
m. his first cousin Mary Jones

7 other children   Ellen (1796-1834)

7 other children

Ven. John Wynne-Jones, Archdeacon of Bangor
(1804-1888)

m. his first cousin Georgiana Wynne-Jones,
of Tralle, Ireland (1819-1901)

5 children
Second cousins to Vincents and Johnsons

Hugh Wynne-Jones (1847-1898)
Went to USA, died in New York

Rev. J.W. (Will) Wynne-Jones (1849-1928)
Vicar of Caernarfon

Robert Wynne-Jones (1850-1915)
Director, Greenall's Brewery

Mary Wynne-Jones (d.1908)
m Joseph Cotterill, Edinburgh surgeon

Georgina (Meg) Wynne-Jones (1856-1934)

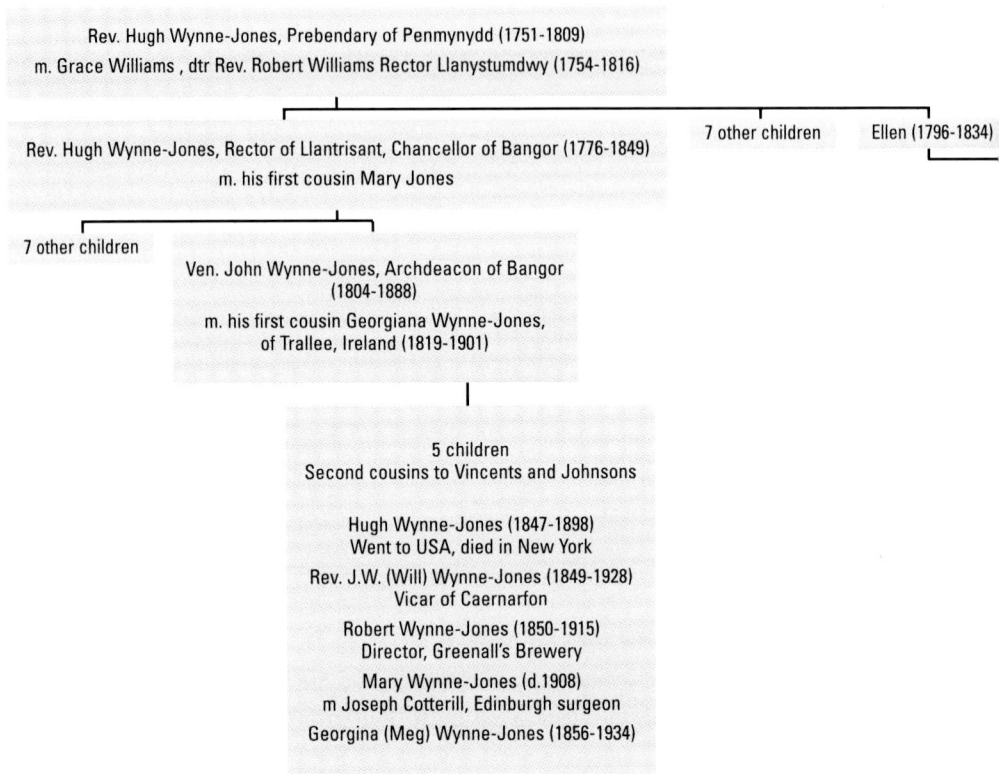

Appendix 5: The Vincent Family descent from
Archbishop Magee of Dublin
(1766-1831) and from Hugh
Wynne-Jones of Treiorwerth
Anglesey (1751-1809)

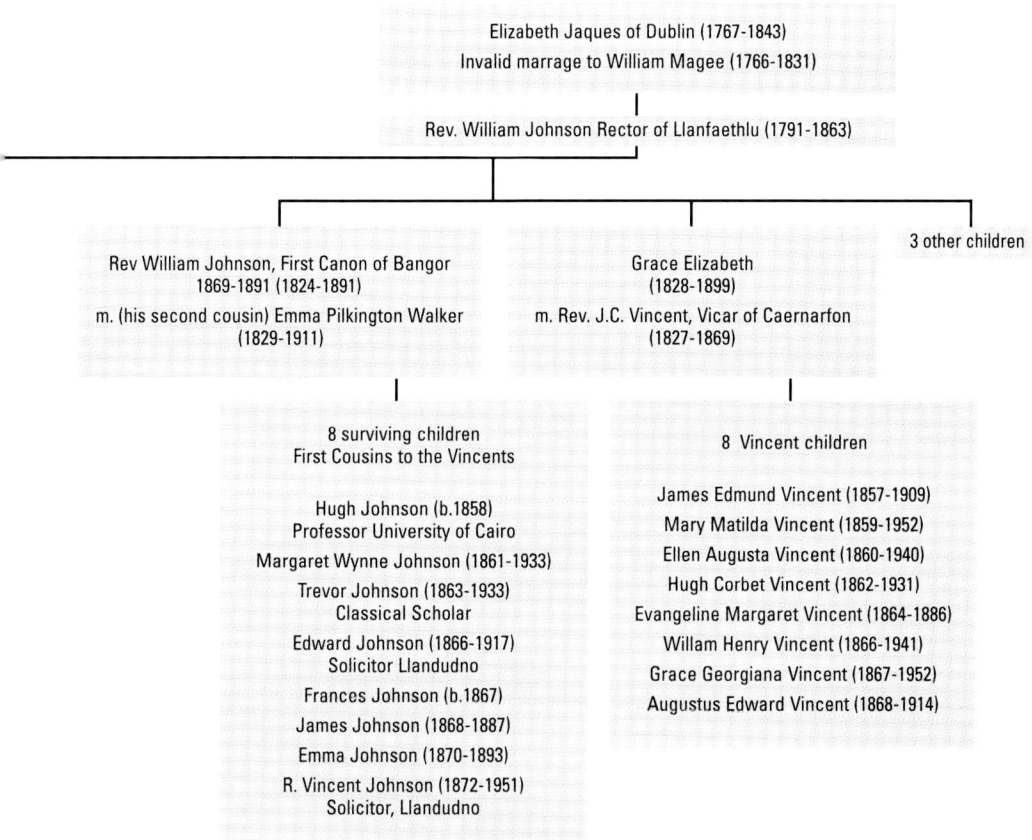

Elizabeth Jaques of Dublin (1767-1843)
Invalid marrage to William Magee (1766-1831)

Rev. William Johnson Rector of Llanfaethlu (1791-1863)

Rev William Johnson, First Canon of Bangor
1869-1891 (1824-1891)
m. (his second cousin) Emma Pilkington Walker
(1829-1911)

Grace Elizabeth
(1828-1899)
m. Rev. J.C. Vincent, Vicar of Caernarfon
(1827-1869)

3 other children

8 surviving children
First Cousins to the Vincents

Hugh Johnson (b.1858)
Professor University of Cairo
Margaret Wynne Johnson (1861-1933)
Trevor Johnson (1863-1933)
Classical Scholar
Edward Johnson (1866-1917)
Solicitor Llandudno
Frances Johnson (b.1867)
James Johnson (1868-1887)
Emma Johnson (1870-1893)
R. Vincent Johnson (1872-1951)
Solicitor, Llandudno

8 Vincent children

James Edmund Vincent (1857-1909)
Mary Matilda Vincent (1859-1952)
Ellen Augusta Vincent (1860-1940)
Hugh Corbet Vincent (1862-1931)
Evangeline Margaret Vincent (1864-1886)
Willam Henry Vincent (1866-1941)
Grace Georgiana Vincent (1867-1952)
Augustus Edward Vincent (1868-1914)